OAK PARK

Danny the Ch
Plays

D0818835

Roald Dahl was born in 1916 in Wales of Norwegian parents. He was educated in England before starting work for the Shell Oil Company in Africa. He began writing after a 'monumental bash on the head' sustained as an RAF fighter pilot during the Second World War. Roald Dahl is one of the most successful and well known of all children's writers. His books, which are read by children the world over, include *James and the Giant Peach*, *Charlie and the Chocolate Factory*, *The Magic Finger*, *Charlie and the Great Glass Elevator*, *Fantastic Mr Fox*, *Matilda*, *The Twits*, *The BFG*, *The Witches*, winner of the 1983 Whitbread Award, and *Danny the Champion of the World*. Roald Dahl died in 1990 at the age of seventy-four.

Roald Dahl

Danny the Champion of the World

plays for Children

Adapted by David Wood

PUFFIN

Find out more about Roald Dahl and the adapted plays by visiting the websites roalddahl.com and davidwood.org.uk

PUFFIN BOOKS

Published by the Penguin Group
Penguin Books Ltd, 80 Strand, London WC2R ORL, England
Penguin Group (USA) Inc., 375 Hudson Street, New York, New York 10014, USA
Penguin Group (Canada), 90 Eglinton Avenue East, Suite 700, Toronto, Ontario, Canada M4P 2Y3
(a division of Pearson Penguin Canada Inc.)
Penguin Ireland, 25 St Stephen's Green, Dublin 2, Ireland (a division of Penguin Books Ltd)
Penguin Group (Australia), 250 Camberwell Road, Camberwell, Victoria 3124, Australia
(a division of Pearson Australia Group Pty Ltd)
Penguin Books India Pvt Ltd, 11 Community Centre, Panchsheel Park, New Delhi – 110 017, India
Penguin Group (NZ), 67 Apollo Drive, Rosedale, North Shore 0632, New Zealand
(a division of Pearson New Zealand Ltd)
Penguin Books (South Africa) (Pty) Ltd, 24 Sturdee Avenue, Rosebank, Johannesburg 2196, South Africa

Penguin Books Ltd, Registered Offices: 80 Strand, London WC2R ORL, England

puffinbooks.com

First published 2009
003

Set in 13/15pt Monotype Baskerville
Typeset by Palimpsest Book Production Ltd, Grangemouth, Stirlingshire
Made and printed in England by Clays Ltd, St Ives plc

British Library Cataloguing in Publication Data
A CIP catalogue record for this book is available from the British Library

ISBN: 978-0-141-32376-3

www.greenpenguin.co.uk

MIX
Paper from
responsible sources
FSC
www.fsc.org   FSC™ C018179

Penguin Books is committed to a sustainable future for our business, our readers and our planet. This book is made from Forest Stewardship Council™ certified paper.

ALWAYS LEARNING   **PEARSON**

CONTENTS

My thanks to Phil Clark and the Sherman Theatre, Cardiff, for commissioning me to adapt the full-length version of *Danny the Champion of the World*, which – following its successful première directed splendidly by Phil – toured all over the UK for Birmingham Stage Company. The play also won the American Alliance for Theatre and Education Best Play (Adaptation) Award, 2007.

David Wood

FOREWORD

Danny the Champion of the World could be considered one of my husband's quietest books; by that, I mean that there are no chocolate factories or giant peaches or friendly giants. And yet, at its heart, the book is quintessentially Roald Dahl, because in it he wrote warmly and movingly about the close bond between a father and son.

Sadly, Roald barely knew his own father, for he died of a broken heart when Roald was very young. Instead, Roald was brought up by his mother, who, like Danny's father, was a strong and loving person, and who left a lasting impression on her son's life.

This is the message of Roald's book. At *Danny*'s conclusion, it calls loudly for parents to be 'SPARKY'! By that Roald meant that grown-ups should remember what it was like to be a child and that stodgy and boring parents were no fun at all.

What Roald might have added was that playwrights should be sparky too! Thank heavens, then, for David Wood. His adaptation of *Danny* is as sparky as ever! I hope that parents (and teachers, and sons and daughters) up and down the land enjoy David's joyous plays as much as I did.

Felicity Dahl

INTRODUCTION

The division of Roald Dahl's classic book into short plays will hopefully prove useful to teachers and youth drama group leaders, both for reading in the classroom and for performing in the school hall or drama festival. It is sometimes said that boys are especially keen on *Danny* because of the strong, warm father–son relationship it portrays. And the lack of magic and fantasy (the effect on pheasants of sleeping powder seems totally plausible!) makes it unique within Dahl's canon of classic stories for children.

My adaptation tries to involve the village community a little more overtly than in the original story. And Sergeant Samways has been made the proud owner of the Austin Seven, which adds a little more dramatic tension when Danny drives it to find his dad. Danny, as is usual with Dahl child protagonists, is far more sensible and reasonable than any of the adults. Thus are the readers, and, hopefully, the audience, empowered; by sometimes using audience participation I have tried to amplify this in the plays. Have fun with them!

David Wood

DREAM COUNTRY

This short play establishes the characters of Danny and his Dad. The opening narration is written for one actor, but could be divided up between several actors if required. The play features Dahl's first mention of the Big Friendly Giant.

CHARACTERS
Narrator

Danny: wearing pyjamas and a sweater round his shoulders.

Dad: wearing a donkey jacket or anorak, a dark sweater, trousers and cloth cap; he carries a bag or sack.

SETTING
To suggest the front of the caravan, a painted cut-out might be best. A picturesque old gypsy caravan would be ideal (see illustration on page 14), but a more modern-looking one would be fine. A couple of steps should lead up to a stable door in the centre or side. The caravan should be positioned in such a way that anyone sitting on the steps can face the audience when performing.

PROPS
An old hunting horn.

Two sandwiches – jam and cheese.

SOUND EFFECTS
An owl hooting. This could be either recorded or created 'live' by a narrator.

LIGHTING
Ideally this would suggest a moonlit night. The area around the door and the steps needs to be bright enough to see the actors. It would be very effective if the glow of a paraffin lamp inside could appear to shine from a caravan window.

DREAM COUNTRY

Curtain up.

DANNY *is sitting on the steps of the caravan, looking anxiously at the road ahead.*

NARRATOR: Danny lives with his father, who runs a small petrol filling station on the edge of a village. Their home is a caravan. It is late at night . . .
[*An owl hoots*]

Danny has woken up. He realizes that his father isn't in the caravan . . .
[DANNY *peers through the darkness. Nothing. He shivers and wraps his sweater tighter round his shoulders*]

[*Pause. Suddenly he hears footsteps. He looks up in anticipation.* DAD *enters, trying to tread softly*]

DANNY: Dad?
[*Relieved, he runs into* DAD*'s arms*]

DAD: Danny! What are you doing up?

DANNY: I thought something awful had happened to you.

DAD: You should be asleep.

DANNY: [*Upset and cross*] Where have you been?

DAD: You must be tired out.

DANNY: I'm not tired. I've been worried.

DAD: I'm sorry.

DANNY: Where have you been, Dad?

DAD: Come on, Danny, back to bed.

[DANNY *sulkily pulls away.* DAD, *feeling guilty, but not wanting to talk further, goes inside the caravan*]

[DANNY *stays outside. Hurt and angry, he sits on the steps. He voices his thoughts to the audience*]

DANNY: I don't get it. What's Dad up to? He left me on my own. Why won't he talk about it? He's never done it before! Maybe he *has*, and I've never woken up before! No, he wouldn't. Would he? Not Dad. He's a great dad. Since Mum died he's had to look after me all on his own, cook the meals, do the washing. He's a great dad, he really is. He teaches me things. Like grasshoppers have their ears, guess where? . . . In the sides of their tummies. But crickets have ears in their legs! He takes me hunting for birds' nests. We found a skylark's once, on the ground in a field, with six tiny eggs, all brown and white. But you mustn't touch them or their mother might abandon them. We made a kite out of some sticks and an old blue shirt. It's got a proper tail and a long string and it flies brilliantly, as long as the wind doesn't drop. Dad's great at making things. Last birthday he built me an amazing car out of bike wheels and old soapboxes. I whizz really fast on it, shooting down the hill. He's a great dad. He smiles with his eyes. All twinkly. You know how some people smile at you with their mouths [*He demonstrates*], but their eyes stay the same. That's not twinkly. Dad's twinkly. [*Pause*] He wasn't so twinkly tonight, though. More like shifty . . .

> [*Suddenly an old hunting horn looms through the curtain covering the top half of the caravan's stable door, accompanied by a loud blowing sound*]

DAD: [*Unseen*] Phooooooooooo!

> [DANNY *jumps, turns and sees the hunting horn pointing at him*]

DANNY: What are you doing?

DAD: [*Acting up well*] I is the BFG!

> [*He pops his head out. He has changed out of his dark sweater*]

I is the Big Friendly Giant. I is a-coming to blow this chiddler a wopsy dream. To cheer him up.

DANNY: [*Resisting joining in the game*] He only does it when the chiddlers are asleep.

DAD: [*In character still*] This chiddler should be asleep. It's very late.

DANNY: Yeah, well.

DAD: [*Coming out of character, but bright, trying to make peace*] Fancy a sandwich? Midnight feast? [*Holding out his hands, a sandwich in each*] Jam or cheese? Cheese or jam?

[DANNY *tries not to show interest*]

It's strawberry.

DANNY: [*Softening a little*] Thanks.
[*He takes the sandwich, and bites into it.* DAD *starts eating the cheese sandwich. Pause*]

DAD: You used to like me being the BFG. Telling you stories about him. [*Gradually getting into skilful storytelling mode*] Striding off to Dream Country, where the dreams mysteriously float around in the air like wispy, misty bubbles. Then he catches them in glass bottles and screws the jars down tight. And, in the dead of night, he goes prowling through the village searching for sleeping children. Because of his great height, he can reach up to their bedroom windows and [*Demonstrating*] blow in the dreams . . .
[DANNY *can't help himself joining in*]

DAD and DANNY: [*Together, a blowing sound*] Phoooooooo!

DAD: And the child begins to dream a . . .
[DANNY *smiles*]

DAD and DANNY: [*Together*] . . . fantastic, delumptious, wopsy dream!
[*Pause.* DANNY*'s smile fades*]

DANNY: Where were you, Dad? You shouldn't just go off like that.

DAD: I was in Dream Country.

DANNY: No, you weren't. What's the big secret? Why won't you tell me?

DAD: I was, Danny. In my very own Dream Country. But it's too late now. I'll tell you tomorrow. Promise. Come on. Busy day tomorrow.
[DANNY *is coaxed inside. The lighting fades*]

[*Curtain down*]

WHAT'S THE BIG SECRET?

This play introduces the community in which Danny and Dad live and work. It involves as many as twenty performers. Some play the villagers, some are puppeteers and some are musicians, who use percussion or their voices to create sound effects. The happy atmosphere as Danny and Dad serve their customers changes to one of menace when the unpleasant Hazell arrives. And Danny is mystified by the strange questions the villagers ask Dad.

CHARACTERS
Narrator

Charlie Kinch, the local taxi-driver: could wear a jacket and jeans.

Dad: wearing overalls.

Danny: wearing jeans and a T-shirt.

Mrs Clipstone, the vicar's wife: wearing a sensible skirt and top.

Sergeant Samways, the village policeman: wearing his uniform.

Hazell, the local landowner: dressed as a country squire.

Several Puppeteers: operate chicken puppets on rods, and should wear dark clothes.

Several Musicians: play percussion instruments and create sound effects such as car horns, a baby crying and chickens clucking.

SETTING

The caravan exterior cut-out, ideally with a door that opens, is upstage centre. On either side, downstage, is a cut-out petrol pump. We can imagine Dad's workshop is offstage. The puppeteers can manipulate the chickens around the petrol pumps.

PROPS

A sign hanging on one of the petrol pumps. It says 'Sorry, closed' on one side and 'Open' on the other.

Chicken puppets on rods.

Three 'cars'. These can be cut-outs on stabilizers. Two should come on from one side and one (the Rolls-Royce) from the other side. The taxi should be a saloon car with a taxi sign on top. The Austin Seven looks old but well looked after.

Coins and banknotes for Mr Kinch and Mrs Clipstone.

A pram for Mrs Clipstone (a large old-fashioned one with a doll baby).

A small soft toy.

An egg box.

A leather riding-crop for Hazell.

Car key on key-ring for Hazell.

A bicycle.

SOUND EFFECTS

Many of the sounds needed could be recorded effects, but it is more fun for the musicians to make them all, using percussion instruments and vocal sounds. Cars starting up or revving their engines, a crying baby or the squawking of chickens should provide an enjoyable challenge to team members who prefer not to act.

LIGHTING

This is a daytime scene, so no special lighting is essential. But it would be effective to start in semi-darkness, and brighten the lights as the sun comes up.

WHAT'S THE BIG SECRET?

Curtain up.

The MUSICIANS *(percussionists and sound-effect makers) sit near the acting area. A drum roll.*

The NARRATOR *steps forward.*

NARRATOR: On the edge of a village, Danny lives in a caravan with his father, who runs a small filling station. It is early one morning.

MUSICIANS: [*A cockerel crows*]

NARRATOR: Only the chickens are awake.
　　[*The* PUPPETEERS *make the chickens enter and peck the ground around the petrol pumps, searching for food*]

MUSICIANS: [*Chickens cluck happily*]

　　[*The* NARRATOR *leaves*]

MUSICIANS: [*Car noise*]

　　[*Enter* CHARLIE*'s taxi. It stops by a petrol pump, scattering the chickens, who exit*]

MUSICIANS: [*Chickens squawk, alarmed*]

　　[CHARLIE *sounds the horn a few times*]

MUSICIANS: [*Car horn noise*]

> [*No reaction*]

> [CHARLIE *gets out of the car and shouts towards the caravan*]

CHARLIE: Shop!
> [DAD *and* DANNY *enter running from the caravan*]

DAD: Sorry, Charlie. Late night!
> [*He changes the 'Sorry, closed' sign to 'Open'*]

CHARLIE: [*Reading significance into this remark*] Aha! No problem, Willum. Mornin', young Danny.

DANNY: Morning, Mr Kinch.

DAD: Danny will look after you, Charlie.

CHARLIE: Okey dokey!
> [DAD *exits to the workshop*]

> [DANNY *operates the pump expertly, carefully inserting the nozzle and turning on the petrol*]

DANNY: Fill her up, Mr Kinch?

CHARLIE: That's it, Danny. Full tank. Long day today. Pick up Mr Pratchett from the airport, then take Mrs Witton to her sister-in-law's, then collect the wife and the shopping from the market.

DANNY: Nice day for it.

CHARLIE: Ah. Warming up nicely. I like September.

DANNY: Do you need oil, Mr Kinch?

CHARLIE: No, no. 'Oi'll' pay for the petrol, then 'Oi'll' be off! Ha, ha!
[DANNY *smiles, hangs the nozzle back on the pump and collects* CHARLIE'*s money*]

DANNY: 'Oi'll' get your change!
[*He goes in the caravan*]

CHARLIE: Ha! Good one!
[DAD *returns from the workshop as the* PUPPETEERS *bring back the chickens*]

MUSICIANS: [*Chickens cluck happily. Occasional clucks continue during the scene*]

CHARLIE: He's bright, your Danny!

DAD: The light of my life, Charlie!

CHARLIE: [*Meaningfully*] Any joy, Willum?

DAD: Eh?
[DANNY *returns, unseen by* DAD *and* CHARLIE. *He overhears their exchange*]

CHARLIE: Last night! Any luck?

DAD: No, not a thing. [*Noticing* DANNY] See you, Charlie, have a good day! [*He exits to the workshop*]

DANNY: Change, Mr Kinch.

CHARLIE: Thanks, Danny. [*Getting in his car*] 'Oi'll' be seeing you! Tata!

MUSICIANS: [*Car starting and leaving; and chickens squawking*]

[CHARLIE *backs the car off. The* PUPPETEERS *make the chickens scatter*]

[*Enter* MRS CLIPSTONE *pushing her pram*]

MUSICIANS: [*Baby crying*]

MRS CLIPSTONE: Hush, Christopher, hush! [*Seeing* DANNY] Good morning, Danny!

DANNY: Hello, Mrs Clipstone!
[*He goes to her*]

MRS CLIPSTONE: Christopher, hush!

MUSICIANS: [*Baby cries more*]

DANNY: [*Looking in the pram*] Hello, Christopher! [*To* MRS CLIPSTONE] How's the vicar?

MRS CLIPSTONE: Fine, thank you, Danny. Writing his sermon for Sunday. I had to come out because Christopher was disturbing his concentration.

MUSICIANS: [*Baby cries louder*]

MRS CLIPSTONE: Christopher!
[DANNY *takes a soft toy from the pram and waves it at the baby*]

DANNY: Chrissy! Chrissy! Chris! Chrissy! Chrissy! Chris! [*Making a funny face*] Dompa dompa dompa dee! Dompa dompa dee! Wheeee!
[*He manipulates the soft toy, playing peep bo with it*]

Boo! Boo!

MUSICIANS: [*Baby stops crying. Happy gurgles*]

DANNY: Yeah! That's better!

MRS CLIPSTONE: You've got the magic touch, Danny. Any time you want to babysit . . .

DANNY: Fine by me, Mrs Clipstone.

MRS CLIPSTONE: Now, have you got any eggs today? [*She hands* DANNY *an egg box*]

DANNY: Eggspect so! I'll have a look.
[*He exits as* DAD *enters*]

[*The* PUPPETEERS *bring back the chickens*]

MUSICIANS: [*Gentle chicken clucks*]

DAD: Mrs Clipstone, good morning!

MRS CLIPSTONE: Hello, William.

DAD: [*Looking in the pram*] Morning, Christopher! [*To* MRS CLIPSTONE] Eggs, is it?

MRS CLIPSTONE: Hope so. Danny's looking. He's a lovely boy, your Danny.

DAD: Thank you, ma'am! I wouldn't disagree with that!

MRS CLIPSTONE: [*Excited*] William, I hear you, er . . . last night.

DAD: Oh. Yes. [*Indicates to* MRS CLIPSTONE *to kindly keep her voice down*]

    [DANNY *enters. He overhears*]

MRS CLIPSTONE: [*Softly*] Any luck?

DAD: No, no! [*Seeing* DANNY] Ah, your eggs, Mrs Clipstone.

MRS CLIPSTONE: Thanks, Danny. [*Paying him*] How's school? Enjoying it?

DANNY: It's all right. But I'd rather be here every day, working with Dad.

MRS CLIPSTONE: Oh. Nothing like a good education. [*Starting to go*] Eh, William?

DAD: Right, Mrs Clipstone. I wish I'd had one! Bye.

MRS CLIPSTONE: [*Leaving*] Bye! Thank you.

DANNY: Bye! Bye, Christopher! [*Deciding to broach the issue*] Dad, what did she mean, 'any luck'?

MUSICIANS: [*The sound of an approaching vehicle*]

DAD: [*Let off the hook*] Hey up! Look, Danny, it's Sergeant Samways in his Austin Seven!

    [*Enter* SERGEANT SAMWAYS *in his vintage Baby Austin. The* PUPPETEERS *make the chickens scatter*]

MUSICIANS: [*The Austin Seven splutters to a halt. Chickens squawk*]

DAD: [*Admiringly*] Nineteen thirty-three . . .

DAD and DANNY: [*Together*] . . . And still running sweet as the proverbial nut!

> [*They happily go to admire the car as* SERGEANT SAMWAYS *climbs out. He is in police uniform, carrying his helmet*]

DAD: Welcome, Sergeant! My favourite customer!

SERGEANT SAMWAYS: [*Laughing*] It's not me you're so pleased to see, William. It's my pride and joy! [*He pats the bonnet affectionately*]

DAD: Always pleased to see you *both.*

SERGEANT SAMWAYS: And 'ow's Danny?

DANNY: Fine, thanks, Sergeant.

DAD: Got a problem?

SERGEANT SAMWAYS: No, no. She's still running sweet as the proverbial nut.

> [DAD *and* DANNY *exchange a quick smile*]

But she's a bit slow starting from cold. Coughing a bit, you know.

DAD: Cylinders might want decarbonizing. We'll fix her up.

SERGEANT SAMWAYS: Much appreciated.

DAD: Our pleasure, eh, Danny?

DANNY: You bet. Can I back her into the workshop, Dad?

DAD: If Sergeant Samways doesn't mind.

SERGEANT SAMWAYS: She's all yours, Danny. I reckon as you knows as much about cars as your dad. Knee-high to a grasshopper you were when you first took an engine to pieces and put it back together again! I'll never forget it. What were you, six?

DANNY: [*Smiling*] Seven.

SERGEANT SAMWAYS: In you get, then.
[DANNY *climbs in*]

Right. Ignition key on. Pull on the choke. Not too much. Right. Now press the starter button.

MUSICIANS: [*The car coughs and dies*]

SERGEANT SAMWAYS: There's the problem, Willum. Try again, Danny.

MUSICIANS: [*The car splutters into life*]

SERGEANT SAMWAYS: That's it. Can you find reverse? [*He looks in to check*] That's the one. Clutch down. A bit of accelerator and off you go!
[*The car starts to reverse*]

MUSICIANS: [*Car reversing sound*]

SERGEANT SAMWAYS: Right hand down a bit! You got it!
[*The car retreats and exits*]

[*The* PUPPETEERS *bring back the chickens*]

MUSICIANS: [*Gentle chicken clucks*]

SERGEANT SAMWAYS: Good lad! [*Quickly, to* DAD] Hey, Willum, a little bird tells me you were out last night . . . success?

DAD: No, 'fraid not, Sergeant, I . . . [*He is interrupted by . . .*]

MUSICIANS: [*The silky sound of an approaching Rolls-Royce*]

DAD: Do you want to borrow my bike?

SERGEANT SAMWAYS: Thank you, Willum. Just till my pride and joy's ready.
  [*They exit*]

  [*Enter, the other side, a Rolls-Royce. At the wheel is* HAZELL, *the local landowner. He parks at the pump. The* PUPPETEERS *make the chickens scatter and exit*]

MUSICIANS: [*The Rolls-Royce arriving, then stopping. Chickens squawking*]

  [*Seeing nobody in attendance,* HAZELL *impatiently sounds his horn several times*]

MUSICIANS: [*Car horn sounds*]

  [HAZELL *steps out of the car, carrying a leather riding-crop*]

DANNY: [*Entering, running*] Sorry to keep you waiting, sir.

HAZELL: [*Throwing* DANNY *the key to the petrol cap*] Fill her up and look sharp about it.

DANNY: Right, sir.

HAZELL: And keep your filthy hands to yourself, d'you understand?

DANNY: What do you mean, sir?
[DAD *enters and listens*]

HAZELL: [*Pointing the riding-crop at* DANNY] If you make any dirty finger-marks on my paintwork, I'll give you a good hiding.
[DAD *steps between* DANNY *and* HAZELL]

DAD: [*Softly, controlling his anger*] I don't like you speaking to my son like that, Mr Hazell.
[HAZELL *avoids* DAD's *gaze, smiling smugly*]

You had no reason to threaten him. He'd done nothing wrong.
[HAZELL *doesn't react*]

Next time you threaten someone with a good hiding, I suggest you pick on a person your own size – like me, for instance. Now go away, please. We do not wish to serve you.
[*He takes the key from* DANNY's *hand and tosses it to* HAZELL]

HAZELL: You'll regret that. No one crosses Victor Hazell and gets away with it. I have friends in very high places. You have been warned.
[*He climbs in the Rolls and starts it*]

MUSICIANS: [*Car starting noise*]

[HAZELL *backs the Rolls off*]

MUSICIANS: [*Car reversing*]

DAD: [*Putting his arm round* DANNY] It's all right, Danny.
[SERGEANT SAMWAYS *enters, pushing* DAD*'s bike*]

SERGEANT SAMWAYS: There goes Mr Charm.

DAD: He makes my blood boil. Just because he got rich
brewing beer he thinks he rules the village. Coming
here and bullying Danny. I'm not a violent man,
Sergeant, but next time I see that great glistening beery
face I'll be sorely tempted to punch its fat nose.

SERGEANT SAMWAYS: I sympathize, Willum. But watch
it. He's a law unto himself, that one. I'll pick up my
pride and joy next week. Bye, Danny.
[*He leaves*]

DANNY: Bye, Sergeant.
[DANNY *watches* DAD, *still furious, exit*]

DANNY: [*Sharing his troubles with the audience*] I've never
seen Dad like this. He's never angry. That Mr
Hazell's horrible, but he didn't hit me. There must
be more to it. What's the big secret?
[DANNY *walks thoughtfully towards the caravan and
steps inside*]

[*Curtain down*]

THE HORSE-HAIR STOPPER
AND THE STICKY HAT

This play is for two actors only; however, a narrator could be used to set the scene. It may prove useful for drama festivals or competitions for duologues. It not only explains the idea of poaching and discusses whether it is morally acceptable, but also celebrates the relationship between father and son. Typically, Dahl makes Danny the more responsible of the two.

CHARACTERS
Danny: wearing jeans and T-shirt.

Dad: dressed similarly until he puts on his donkey jacket and cap to go poaching.

A Narrator sets the scene if necessary.

SETTING
The interior of the caravan. Essential are a table and two chairs and a door at the back. Two bunks would help create the homely atmosphere.

PROPS
A paraffin lamp.

A paraffin burner, saucepan, spoon, baked beans.

Two plates, cutlery.

A kettle.

Two mugs, cocoa and sugar tins, spoons.

A jar of raisins.

A torch.

Large envelope, scissors.

A hand-puppet chicken.

Dad's poaching sack.

SOUND EFFECTS
Chickens squawking and clucking.

A kettle whistling as it comes to the boil.

LIGHTING
The paraffin lamp could create a cosy atmosphere. The scene takes place in the evening. If the caravan interior could sit in an isolated pool of light, it would help the intimacy of the scene.

THE HORSE-HAIR STOPPER AND THE STICKY HAT

Curtain up.

Early evening. A paraffin lamp illuminates the table where DANNY *and* DAD *sit eating.*

NARRATOR: Last night Danny was very worried when he woke up late to find his father missing. He eventually returned to their caravan, but with no proper explanation. Danny is still upset.

DAD: More baked beans?

DANNY: Please.
    [DAD *goes to the paraffin burner, picks up the saucepan and spoons out some baked beans on to* DANNY*'s plate. Then he puts the kettle on the burner.* DANNY *eats in silence*]

DAD: Danny, about last night.

DANNY: Where were you, Dad? What's the big secret?

DAD: I was up in Hazell's Wood.

DANNY: Hazell's Wood! That's miles away!

DAD: Six miles and a half. I know I shouldn't have gone, and I'm very, very sorry about it. But I had such a powerful yearning . . .

DANNY: What's so special about Hazell's Wood?
[DAD *spoons cocoa and sugar into two mugs*]

DAD: Danny, do you know what is meant by poaching?

DANNY: Poaching? Not really, no. Except poaching eggs.

DAD: It means going up into the woods in the dead of night and coming back with something for the pot. Something to eat. Poachers in other places poach all sorts of different things, but around here it's always pheasants. Lovely birds. Tasty too.

DANNY: You mean *stealing* them? Poaching is stealing?

DAD: No. Poaching is an art. That's how we country folk see it. A poacher is a great artist.

DANNY: So you were stealing pheasants in Hazell's Wood?

DAD: I was practising the art of poaching. Not very successfully, as it turned out.

DANNY: Who do the pheasants belong to?

DAD: Mr Hazell.

DANNY: What, the man in the Rolls?
[DAD *nods.* DANNY *is shocked*]

The kettle's boiling.
[DAD *fetches the kettle, and pours water into the mugs. He turns off the paraffin burner, sits and stirs the mugs, then hands one to* DANNY]

DAD: Cocoa.

DANNY: [*Quietly*] Thanks.

DAD: Your grandad, my own dad, was a magnificent and splendiferous poacher. He taught me all about it when I was ten years old. I caught the poaching fever from him and I've never lost it since. When I was a boy, times were bad for a lot of people. There was very little work to be had anywhere and some families were literally starving. Yet a few minutes away in the rich man's wood, thousands of pheasants were being fed like kings twice a day. So can you blame my dad for going out occasionally and coming home with a bird or two for the family to eat?

DANNY: No, of course not. But *we're* not starving, Dad.

DAD: You're missing the point, Danny boy! Poaching is such a fabulous and exciting sport that once you start doing it, it gets into your blood and you can't give it up! Just imagine . . . [*He leaps up and graphically paints the scene*] . . . you are all alone up there in the dark wood, and the wood is full of keepers hiding behind the trees. And the keepers have guns . . .

DANNY: Guns! They don't have guns!

DAD: All keepers have guns, Danny. To shoot the vermin, mostly. But they'll always take a pot at a poacher too, if they spot him.

DANNY: Dad, you're having me on!

DAD: I'm serious! But they only do it from behind. Only when you're trying to escape. They like to pepper you in the legs at about fifty yards.

DANNY: They can't do that! They could go to prison for shooting someone.

DAD: You could go to prison for poaching! Many's the night when I was a boy, Danny, I've gone into the kitchen and seen my old dad lying face down on the table . . . go on, you be my dad! Over the table!
[DANNY *smiles and bends over the table*]

That's it. And I'll be my mum! She used to stand over him digging the gunshot pellets out of his backside with a potato-knife!
[*He demonstrates on* DANNY]

DANNY: [*Laughing*] It's not true!

DAD: You don't believe me? [*He tickles* DANNY]

DANNY: [*Laughing more*] I believe you!

DAD: Towards the end, he was so covered in tiny little white scars he looked exactly like it was snowing.

DANNY: I don't know why I'm laughing. It's not funny. It's horrible.
[*He sits again*]

DAD: 'Poacher's Bottom', they used to call it.

DANNY: 'Poacher's Bottom'!

DAD: And there wasn't a man in the whole village who didn't have a bit of it one way or another. But my dad was the champion. Drink your cocoa!

[DANNY *takes a sip*]

DANNY: So last night you were poaching Mr Hazell's pheasants.

DAD: Trying to. Last night was the first time for nine years. Since your mother died. You see, I made a vow I'd never do it again till you were old enough to be left alone. But last night I had this tremendous longing. I just couldn't stop myself. I'm sorry.

DANNY: You might have got 'Poacher's Bottom'.

DAD: I was very careful.

DANNY: But why does Mr Hazell *have* all these pheasants? With keepers guarding them?

DAD: Good question. Wealthy idiots like *Mister* Hazell rear pheasants just for the fun of shooting them down when they grow up. They call it sport.

DANNY: Is that why you don't like Mr Hazell?

DAD: [*Carefully*] That's the main reason, yes.

DANNY: But *you* kill the pheasants too.

DAD: Not for the cold-blooded fun of it! I've told you, poaching's an art. And a real poacher never shoots a pheasant, never uses a gun.

DANNY: How do you do it then?

DAD: Ah. These things are big secrets. Very big secrets indeed. But I reckon if my father could tell them to me, then maybe I can tell them to you.

DANNY: Yes, please.

DAD: First big secret. [*Confidentially*] Raisins. [*He finds some to show* DANNY]

DANNY: Raisins.

DAD: Ordinary raisins. My old dad discovered that pheasants are crazy about raisins. Throw them a few and they'll fight over them.

DANNY: And then you grab them?

DAD: No, no. Far too noisy. They'd squawk and flap. And the keepers would hear. Listen. Next big secret. My old dad's Method for Catching Pheasants Number One. The Horse-hair Stopper.

DANNY: The Horse-hair Stopper.

DAD: Right. You soak a few raisins in water overnight to make them plump and juicy, then push in a half-inch length of horse-hair. You leave a little bit sticking out on each side of the raisins. That's all you do.

DANNY: Then what?

DAD: When evening comes, you creep up into the woods, making sure you get there before the pheasants have gone into the trees to roost. Then you scatter the raisins. And soon, along comes a pheasant and gobbles one up. Then, and this was my dad's great discovery, the horse-hair makes the raisin stick in the pheasant's throat. It doesn't hurt him; it simply stays there and tickles. But after that, believe it or not, the pheasant never moves his feet again! He's rooted to the spot! And there he stands, pumping his silly neck up and down like a piston. All you have to do is quickly nip out of hiding and pick him up!

DANNY: Really?

DAD: I swear it! It's brilliant! My dad was a genius to discover that. Method Number One.

DANNY: What's Method Number Two?

DAD: Ah. Number Two's a real beauty! Dad called it 'The Sticky Hat'. I remember him trying it out on a huge white rooster from the backyard.

DANNY: [*Having an idea*] Would it work on a chicken?

DAD: Don't see why not.
[DANNY *jumps up and goes to open the door*]

[*Laughing*] Take the torch!

[DANNY *goes out of the caravan shining a torch. We hear chickens squawking*]

[DAD *cuts the corner off an old envelope*]

[DANNY *returns holding a chicken (a puppet, which he manipulates)*]

DAD: I remember when Dad brought in the rooster – Mum had a fit! 'Horace,' she shouts, 'take that filthy bird off my table!'
[DANNY *holds the chicken. Its head darts up and down. Clucking noises*]

But then he showed her 'The Sticky Hat' and she soon calmed down.

DANNY: Go on, then. Show me.

DAD: Right. Dad had discovered that if you put a paper hat over a pheasant's head . . .
[*He pops the envelope corner over the chicken's head. The chicken immediately stops moving and clucking*]

. . . See?

DANNY: She's gone all still!

DAD: Exactly! Cover its eyes and no bird'll run away. You just pick him up! And Bob's your uncle! One for the pot!
[*He removes the hat and the chicken starts moving and clucking again. Then he pops the hat back. The chicken is still again*]

DANNY: That's brilliant. But why's it called 'The Sticky Hat'?

DAD: Well, you put a little smear of glue inside, then press it into the ground and pop a raisin or two inside. Then you lay a trail of raisins along the ground leading up to it. Pheasant comes along, pecks away, pops his head in the hat, the glue sticks, head up and . . .

DAD and DANNY: [*Together*] Bob's your uncle! One for the pot!

DANNY: Did you use 'The Sticky Hat' last night?

DAD: I was going to. But I got there too late. The pheasants were already going up to roost. That shows you how out of practice I am.

DANNY: If you ever want to go again, I won't mind, Dad.

DAD: Do you mean that? No, no, it's unfair . . .

DANNY: As long as you tell me beforehand. And as long as you don't get 'Poacher's Bottom'!

DAD: You sure you won't mind? If I promise to tell you.

DANNY: No. [*Pause*] Go tonight if you like.

DAD: Really? No, I . . .

DANNY: Go on.

DAD: [*Tempted*] Well, it's a long walk . . . but there might just be time . . .

DANNY: Well, then. [*Idea*] And I could come too.

DAD: Ah.

DANNY: We'd make a good team.

DAD: Well, I reckon you're just a bit young to be dodging around up there in the dark.

DANNY: Your dad took you at my age, didn't he?

DAD: Well, one day, eh? But I'd like to get back into practice before I make any promises, you understand?

DANNY: Yes.

DAD: [*Meaningfully*] Thanks, Danny.
[*He removes the paper cap from the chicken*]

You'd better put her back.
[DANNY *nods and takes the chicken from the caravan.*]

[DAD *puts on his donkey jacket and picks up a sack*]

[DANNY *returns*]

Are you sure about this?

DANNY: Of course. Good luck!

DAD: Thanks, Danny. And don't stay up late. I'll be back by half-past ten at the latest. Promise.
[*They hug*]

[DAD *puts on his cloth cap, leaves the caravan and exits*]

DANNY: [*Sharing his thoughts with the audience*] Well, it's only fair he has his fun. But that poaching's a bit of an eye-opener. I had no idea. At least he's told me about it.

[*He yawns, then sees the envelope corner and picks it up*]

[*With a smile*] The Sticky Hat! You'd never think that would work.

[*He yawns*]

Happy hunting, Dad.

[DANNY *nods off to sleep*]

[*Curtain down*]

DANNY TO THE RESCUE

Five actors and a narrator perform this play, which needs some special lighting effects, including car headlamps. Danny drives the Austin Seven and rescues his father from a mantrap.

CHARACTERS
Narrator

Danny: wearing his T-shirt and jeans, a sweater round his shoulders.

Dad: wearing his donkey jacket, jeans and cap.

Two Gamekeepers: wearing boots and waterproof clothing and headgear. One of these characters is Rabbetts, Hazell's head gamekeeper. The other will be named simply 'Gamekeeper' in this play.

Hazell: wearing his country squire clothes.

SETTING
An empty space surrounded by black curtains.

Danny can 'sleep' on the bare stage; there is no need to see the caravan.

If there is no trapdoor in your stage for the mantrap, Dad can emerge from behind the bottom of a curtain.

PROPS
Three torches.

Two shotguns.

Tow-rope.

The Austin Seven could be created from an office chair on castors or a pedal car. Danny needs to be able to sit and 'drive' the car. Ideally, the headlamps can be turned on and off.

SOUND EFFECTS
The car sounds – engine starting and running – and the police-car siren could be recorded or created vocally offstage.

It would be effective if Dad's voice, when coming from the mantrap, echoed a little.

LIGHTING
The whole scene takes place in moonlight, but we need to see the actors' faces!

A flashing blue light could suggest a passing police car.

DANNY TO THE RESCUE

Curtain up.

NARRATOR: Late at night, Danny is alone, asleep. His father has gone poaching in Hazell's Wood. Earlier in the day, Sergeant Samways brought his pride and joy, his Austin Seven motor car, to be repaired by Danny's father.

[DANNY *wakes with a start*]

DANNY: Dad?

[*He looks around, but there is no sign of* DAD. *He peers at his watch*]

Ten past two! Oh, Dad. Half-past ten at the latest, you promised. Where are you? What's happened? What if he's lying in Hazell's Wood, bleeding to death? No, don't be silly. But where is he?

[*He makes a decision*]

Right, Dad. I'm coming to find you.

[*He puts on his sweater*]

Torch.

[*He finds it, then sets off*]

[*Suddenly stopping*] But it's six and a half miles! It'll take ages to get there. Should I phone the police? No, that's stupid. They might put Dad in prison.

[*Having a sudden idea and shining the torch towards the car*]

Maybe I could . . . no, I couldn't . . . Why not? It's an emergency! . . . Go on then!

[DANNY *goes to the car and gets in. The headlamps light up*]

[*A cough from the engine. Another cough*]

Come on, pride and joy, *please*.

[*The car splutters into life*]

Clutch. First gear. Clutch and accelerator. Hang on, Dad. I'm on my way.

[*Slowly the car travels to centre stage, and stops, facing the audience.* DANNY *concentrates hard behind the wheel. The noise of the engine increases as he goes into second gear and drives (on the spot) towards Hazell's Wood*]

[*Suddenly headlamps shine in* DANNY'*s eyes, as we hear a car approaching towards him. Noise and light increase.* DANNY *is dazzled. The car flashes past and speeds away*]

DANNY: Police! [*Suddenly realizing*] It might be Sergeant Samways! And I'm in his pride and joy! He might have seen me!

[*He drives on. In the distance a police siren wails*]

He's coming back!

[DANNY *turns the wheel, as though to stop at the side of the road, turns off the headlamps and sits in the darkness*]

[*The noise of the police-car engine and siren approaches, the car zooms past, and the sounds recede*]

[DANNY, *relieved, after a pause, turns on the headlamps again and drives on*]

[*He arrives at Hazell's Wood and parks the car to one side. He turns off the headlamps, gets out of the car, turns on his torch, then nervously advances into the wood*]

DANNY: [*Trying not to call too loudly*] Dad! Dad! Are you there?
[*No reaction. More searching*]

Dad! It's Danny! Please tell me where you are! Please answer! Dad!
[*He stands still to listen for a reaction. None comes. More searching as* DANNY *moves further into the wood*]

Dad!
[*Suddenly a muffled sound halts* DANNY *in his tracks*]

DAD: Here!
[DANNY *listens*]

Over here!

DANNY: [*Looking around*] Dad?

DAD: [*A little louder*] Danny? I'm here.

DANNY: [*Trying to place the sound*] I'm coming, Dad.
[*He walks carefully forward, shining the torch. Suddenly . . .*]

DAD: Stop, Danny, stop!
[DANNY *stops, but can't see* DAD]

DANNY: Where are you?

DAD: Down here. Come forward slowly.
[DANNY *edges forward*]

Careful! Don't fall in! It's a pit. A mantrap.
[DANNY *finds the pit, kneels, and shines the torch down. We can't see* DAD]

DANNY: Oh, Dad.

DAD: Hello, my marvellous darling. Thank you for coming.

DANNY: Did they dig the hole to catch people?

DAD: Yes. And I was stupid enough to fall in.

DANNY: Are you all right?

DAD: I think I've broken my ankle.
[*Two torchlight beams appear from offstage*]

DANNY: Does it hurt?
[*Enter* GAMEKEEPERS 1 *and* 2]

GAMEKEEPER 1: That way, quick.

DAD: Yes, it hurts a lot. But don't worry about that. The point is . . .
[DANNY *suddenly sees the approaching* GAMEKEEPERS]

DANNY: [*Urgently*] Shut up, Dad!
[DANNY *quickly snaps off his torch and runs to hide*]

DAD: . . . Eh, what's up?

> [*The* GAMEKEEPERS *arrive. They shine a torch down the pit*]

RABBETTS: Well, well, well! I thought I heard something!

GAMEKEEPER: The squeal of dirty, stinking vermin.

RABBETTS: Look at it. Skulking like a cornered rat!

GAMEKEEPER: Come on, show us your miserable, weaselly face.

RABBETTS: Oh, shy, are we?

GAMEKEEPER: I'll pepper it with shot. That'll shift it.
> [*He raises his shotgun*]

RABBETTS: No, no. We'll leave him here to stew. The boss can find out who he is.

GAMEKEEPER: Yeah. Hey, vermin! Guess who's coming back with us to fish you out?

RABBETTS: Mr Victor Hazell himself, to say hello to you.

GAMEKEEPER: And he hates poachers.

RABBETTS: I hate to think what he'll do when he gets his hands on you! Scum!
> [*He hawks and spits down the pit, then, laughing, the* GAMEKEEPERS *exit through the trees*]

[DANNY *emerges from hiding, then tentatively returns to the pit. He shines the torch*]

DANNY: Come on, Dad. Got to get you out before they come back. [*Stretching down*] Hold my hand.

DAD: Thanks, Danny.
[*With a great effort, using both hands,* DANNY *pulls till* DAD*'s head appears*]

Ow! Hang on!
[*One hand clings on to the edge*]

DANNY: Have a rest, Dad.

DAD: [*In pain*] I don't think . . . Ah! . . . My ankle, Danny. I'll never be able to walk back.

DANNY: Dad, I brought the car! Sergeant Samways' pride and joy.

DAD: You *what?*
[*He falls back into the pit*]

Ow!

DANNY: I wanted to get here quickly!

DAD: You're crazy. You might have been killed.

DANNY: Well, I wasn't. Come on [*Stretching down*], try again.

DAD: [*Straining*] You're amazing, Danny.

DANNY: Come on, up!

[DAD*'s head appears again*]

DAD: Thank you!
[*But again he falls back*]

Ow! It's no good. I'll never get out of here without a ladder.

DANNY: What about a rope?

DAD: Well, yes, but we haven't got a rope.

DANNY: There's a tow-rope in the car.

DAD: Brilliant!

DANNY: Stay there!
[*He runs towards the car*]

DAD: I haven't much choice!
[DANNY *finds the tow-rope, attaches it to the tow-bar, then takes the other end and throws it down the pit. He returns to the car, starts it, then drives slowly forward, pulling* DAD *out of the pit.* DAD *tries to stand, but cannot.* DANNY *helps him hop to the passenger seat and climb in. Then* DANNY *collects the rope, gets in the car and, turning on the headlamps, drives offstage*]

[*After a pause, the* GAMEKEEPERS *enter, gleefully leading* HAZELL *to the pit.* HAZELL *rubs his hands in anticipation*]

HAZELL: Good work! I told you a pit would do the trick. [*Shouting down the pit*] Hey, you worm. I'll make you squirm, thieving little parasite! Poaching deserves punishment and punished you will be! [*To the* GAMEKEEPERS] Torch! Shotgun! [*The* GAMEKEEPERS *both pass him a torch*] No! You shine the torch! Give me the shotgun!

[*The* GAMEKEEPERS *shine the torches down the pit.* HAZELL *cocks the shotgun and takes aim. He moves the shotgun as he scans the pit*]

[*Realizing*] What! What! Ahhhh! You idiots! Fools! Imbeciles! He's escaped!

[*He angrily pushes* RABBETTS *and the* GAMEKEEPER. *The* GAMEKEEPER *drops his torch in the pit. He bends to look for it*]

Stupid! Dunderheads! Grrrrh!

[HAZELL *pushes the* GAMEKEEPER *into the pit*]

GAMEKEEPER: Aaaaaaaah!

[RABBETTS *beats a hasty retreat*]

HAZELL: Hey! You! [*Chasing* RABBETTS *offstage*] Come back! Come back!

[*Curtain down*]

WHILE DAD'S AWAY . . .

With four principal roles, plus opportunities for puppeteers and one or several musicians, this play is in three scenes, linked by the Narrator. To balance the male/female roles in the play I suggest that Doctor Spencer (male in the book) be female. The Council Inspector (a character not featured in the book) is also female in the play. Both roles could, of course, be male.

CHARACTERS
Narrator

Dad: wearing his poaching gear – sweater and jeans; one leg of the jeans needs to split to the knee.

Doctor Spencer: wearing country tweeds.

Danny: wearing jeans and T-shirt.

Council Inspector: wearing a smart suit, with muddy shoes.

One or two Ambulance Men: wearing uniform.

Several Puppeteers: operate chicken puppets on rods, and should wear dark clothes.

One or more Musicians to link the scenes.

SETTING

The caravan exterior cut-out, with opening door. Ideally there would be steps leading up to the door, but this is not essential.

Two stools or chairs.

Two cut-out petrol pumps, one either side.

PROPS

Blanket.

Doctor Spencer's medical bag.

Scissors.

Two pieces of wood to make a splint.

Bandage.

Bottle of sleeping pills.

Wheelchair (or stretcher).

Puppet chickens on rods.

Clipboard.

Badge for Council Inspector.

Crutch.

Plaster cast.

Two plates with cutlery.

SOUND EFFECTS

The sound of the approaching ambulance could be made by the Musicians.

The chicken clucks and squawks should be made by the Puppeteers.

Music could open the play. Between each scene, percussion instruments could provide 'time passing' tick-tocks.

LIGHTING

No special lighting is required, but for the third (evening) scene, it would be effective to fade the lighting, and to perhaps have paraffin lamps to give atmosphere.

WHILE DAD'S AWAY . . .

Curtain up.

MUSICIANS: [*Optional music*]

> [DAD *is lying on a blanket in front of the caravan, propped up against the steps.* DOCTOR SPENCER *is attending him*]

NARRATOR: His father has shared with Danny his Big Secret – he poaches pheasants from Hazell's Wood. But one night he falls down Mr Hazell's mantrap. Danny bravely rescues him.

DOCTOR SPENCER: But great heavens alive! He can't do that! Victor Hazell can't go digging tiger-traps in the woods for human beings. It's monstrous!

DAD: Monstrous, yes, Doctor. Hazell's a monster, all right.

DOCTOR SPENCER: [*Pressing* DAD*'s ankle*] Does that hurt, William?

DAD: Ooh! Yes.

DOCTOR SPENCER: Not surprised. It's broken all right.
> [*Enter* DANNY]

DANNY: I phoned the hospital, Doctor Spencer. The ambulance is on its way.

DOCTOR SPENCER: Well done, Danny. And well done rescuing your dad.

DAD: Couldn't have got out without him.

DOCTOR SPENCER: Hand me those scissors, please, Danny. In my bag.
[DANNY *does so.* DOCTOR SPENCER *attacks* DAD'*s trouser leg*]

It's diabolical, William. Thanks, Danny. It means that decent folk like you and me can't even go out and have a little, er . . . 'fun' at night without risking a broken leg or arm. We might even break our necks! Hold still, William.

DANNY: [*Incredulous*] You don't mean . . . *you* surely don't do it too, Doctor Spencer?

DOCTOR SPENCER: Well, I have been known to indulge in a bit of [*Whispering the word*] poaching, Danny. Great fun. Tickling the odd trout.

DANNY: Tickling them?

DOCTOR SPENCER: Trout love a little tickle! Doze off, they do. Then you can flip 'em out of the water.

DANNY: Really?

DAD: Not as easy as it sounds. I've tried!

DOCTOR SPENCER: You were always better at pheasants, William. Where's that splint?
[*Finds it and starts applying it*]

I was never much good with pheasants. Lie still, William.

DANNY: What method did you use?

DOCTOR SPENCER: Raisins soaked in gin. Meant to make the pheasants tiddly! Doesn't work!
[DAD *laughs*]

Keep still, William.

DAD: They have to eat at least sixteen gin-soaked raisins before they get tiddly. My old dad tried it out with roosters.

DANNY: Dad uses The Sticky Hat.

DOCTOR SPENCER: Ah! [*Admiringly*] The Sticky Hat!

DAD: Didn't get a chance tonight, thanks to Hazell's trap.

DOCTOR SPENCER: I never did like that Victor Hazell. He needed an injection once. I saw him through the window, driving up to the surgery in his whacking great Rolls. My old dog, Bertie, was dozing on the doorstep, and – would you believe it – Hazell didn't step over him, he kicked him out of the way with his riding-boot.

DAD: He didn't!

DOCTOR SPENCER: [*Finishing off the splint*] He did, the brute.

DANNY: What did you do?

DOCTOR SPENCER: I left him sitting in the waiting-room while I picked out the oldest, bluntest needle I could find. Then I rubbed the point of it on a nail-file to make it blunter still. By the time I'd got through with it, it was blunter than a ball-point pen. Then I called him in and told him to lower his pants and bend over. Go on, Danny, you be Hazell.

[DANNY *smiles and bends over.* DOCTOR SPENCER *demonstrates*]

Then I rammed the needle into his fleshy backside and he screamed like a stuck pig!

[DANNY *enjoys screaming.* DAD *laughs*]

DAD: Hooray!

[*Distant sounds of the ambulance approaching*]

DOCTOR SPENCER: He's never been back since. For which I'm truly thankful. Ah, here's the ambulance. Now, Danny . . . [*Taking a bottle of pills from the bag, and handing them to* DANNY] . . . look after these for when your dad gets home. Sleeping pills. He might need them.

DANNY: Thanks, Doctor Spencer.

[*Two* AMBULANCE MEN *enter with a wheelchair and help* DAD *into it*]

DOCTOR SPENCER: [*Confidentially leaning down to talk to* DAD] And William, seriously, don't start planning revenge on Hazell. He's a nasty piece of work, no

mistake, but don't push him too far. He might . . .
You know what I'm talking about.

DAD: Yeah, yeah!

DOCTOR SPENCER: Right, let's go.
[DANNY *watches as* DAD *is pushed off*]

DAD: See you later, Danny.

DANNY: Good luck, Dad.
[PUPPETEERS *bring chickens in the other side. They
cluck around the petrol pump*]

[DANNY *shares his thoughts with the audience and the
chickens, which he feeds as he speaks*]

What did Doctor Spencer mean? 'He might . . . You
know what I'm talking about'? *I* don't know what
she's talking about. Hazell might what? [*He sighs*]
Another big secret.
[*He throws some chicken feed behind the petrol pump. The
chickens exit, clucking, in pursuit*]

[DANNY *looks at the sleeping pills and decides to put them
in the caravan. He goes in*]

MUSICIANS: [*Tick-tock sounds to suggest the passing of time*]

NARRATOR: That afternoon, when his Dad is still at
the hospital, Danny receives an unexpected visitor.
[*Suddenly squawking chickens flutter from behind the pump.*
DANNY *comes out of the caravan to investigate. He meets
the* COUNCIL INSPECTOR, *who enters hurriedly, avoiding*

*the chickens. She is fastidiously dressed. Her smart shoes
are muddy. She carries a clipboard. During the scene, the
chickens, clucking softly, peck round the petrol pump]*

DANNY: What's going on?

INSPECTOR: Sorry, dear. I just popped round the back
and met your wildly free-range chickens. Bit muddy
round there.

DANNY: [*Not pleased*] Can I help you?

INSPECTOR: I hope so, dear. [*Showing a badge*] I'm from
the Council. Is your mum in?

DANNY: No, she's dead.

INSPECTOR: Oh, I am sorry. [*Looking at the clipboard*]
Silly me. I mean is your dad in?

DANNY: No, he's . . . [*Deciding not to mention the hospital*]
. . . out.

INSPECTOR: Are you on your own?

DANNY: Yes.

INSPECTOR: Shouldn't you be at school?

DANNY: Well, maybe. But I'm looking after the filling
station till Dad gets back. [*Reluctantly*] He's at the
hospital.

INSPECTOR: [*Making notes*] Mmm. I see. Well, maybe
you could just show me the caravan.

DANNY: Why?

INSPECTOR: Just to check it's a fit place for humans to live in.

DANNY: What do you mean?

INSPECTOR: [*Brightly*] We don't allow people to live in dirty broken-down shacks these days.

DANNY: It's not dirty! Or broken-down! It's my home!

INSPECTOR: Of course, dear. I'm only joking. Can I have a peep inside?

DANNY: S'pose so.
[*The* INSPECTOR *climbs the steps and looks inside*]

INSPECTOR: Mmm. Very snug. Sleep in here, do you?

DANNY: Of course.

INSPECTOR: And eat? How do you cook?

DANNY: Paraffin burner.

INSPECTOR: I see. No electricity then?

DANNY: Not in here, no.

INSPECTOR: What about light? How do you see to do your homework?

DANNY: Paraffin lamp.

INSPECTOR: Ah, yes. I can smell it. [*Coming down the steps*] Do you wash, dear?

DANNY: Of course.

INSPECTOR: I can't see a bath!

DANNY: Dad heats a kettle of water, then gives me a good scrub standing up. Don't need a bath.
[*The chickens squawk and strut*]

INSPECTOR: No. I see. [*Making notes*] Good. Well, thank you, dear. That's all I need. Do these chickens always run around like this? Good morning.
[DANNY *watches her leave, treading carefully through the chickens, who follow her off. He is worried*]

DANNY: [*To the chickens and the audience*] What was that all about? What did she want? [*Imitating the* INSPECTOR] How do you have a bath? Do the chickens always run around like this? [*Answering as a chicken*] Cluck, cluck, yes, well actually we do, your ladyship, cluck, cluck, cos we live here, cluck, cluck. [*As* DANNY] Better tell Dad tonight.
[*He goes in the caravan. Perhaps the lighting fades to suggest evening*]

MUSICIANS: [*Tick-tock sounds to suggest the passing of time*]

NARRATOR: That evening, when Dad has returned from the hospital . . .
[*Enter* DAD, *hobbling with a crutch, a plaster cast on his leg*]

. . . Danny cooks him a meal . . .
[DANNY *carries plates from the caravan.* DAD *and*

DANNY *sit and eat*]

. . . then tells him about today's visitor . . .

DAD: [*Very cross*] How dare they send someone round to snoop on us? Saying it's dirty in here!

DANNY: She said that bit was a joke.

DAD: Bloomin' cheek. Before your mum died I promised her I'd look after you properly.

DANNY: And you do, Dad.

DAD: I do the washing – I used to wash your nappies, I scrub the floor, change the sheets every week, and now you're older, you do your bit. It's spotless in here! How dare they?

DANNY: More baked beans, Dad?

DAD: No thanks, Danny. That was great. You're a great help! I'm proud of you.

DANNY: [*Clearing the plates*] How's the ankle?

DAD: Hardly hurts at all. [*Standing to prove it and stamping his foot*] Ow! Well, maybe just a little. And it itches under the plaster!

DANNY: You'd better have a sleeping pill.

DAD: No need. I'll sleep like a top.
[DANNY *takes the plates into the caravan*]

Dirty, she said. I don't believe it. [*Thinking*] Wouldn't mind betting Hazell's behind this.

DANNY: [*Returning*] Hazell? No, it was the Council.

DAD: But who put the Council up to it? Eh? Hazell. Just the sort of mean trick that fat slug would pull. One day I'll get him, you wait.

DANNY: Careful, Dad.

DAD: What?

DANNY: I heard Doctor Spencer warn you about Mr Hazell. About not trying to get revenge. She said Hazell might do something. She said you knew what she meant. And you said yes, you knew what she meant. But *I* don't know! *I* don't know what she meant! I'm always the last to know. It's another silly Big Secret you don't share with me! And I don't like it! It's not fair! It sounds very serious and I'm just left in the dark. What might Mr Hazell do? Tell me! How can I help when I don't know what the hell is going on?

[DANNY *is near to tears, having exploded for the first time*]

[*Silence*]

DAD: You're right, Danny. You're always right. I shouldn't hide things from you. I wanted to protect you, but I've ended up getting you worried. What do you want to know?

DANNY: Why do you hate Hazell so much? It's not just his money or that he's rude. There must be something more. What's the big secret?

DAD: [*Nodding*] He's a roaring snob and he's very nasty, but yes, there's more. He owns all the land for miles around. Not just the wood – everything on either side of the valley. Everything except this little patch where we live. The filling station and the caravan.

DANNY: Who owns this bit?

DAD: We do. But Mr Hazell wants it. Nothing would please him more than to get his podgy hands on it. And greedy men like Hazell are ruthless. They won't live and let live. They stop at nothing to get their way. Nothing, Danny. Nothing.

[*Curtain down*]

HAZELL COMES TO SCHOOL

The fun of this play is that most of it takes place at a school assembly. So the audience 'play' the schoolchildren. Danny and Hazell have a dramatic confrontation, and the Headteacher punishes Danny in a manner which couldn't happen these days. The acceptability of corporal punishment is questioned by Dad.

CHARACTERS
Narrator

Choir: who sit with the audience.

Headteacher: possibly wearing gown and mortarboard, to signal the fact that we are in the 1950s; this role could be male or female.

Mr Jackson, another teacher: could be the games teacher, wearing a tracksuit.

Hazell: wearing his gentleman farmer gear.

Rabbetts, Hazell's head gamekeeper: wearing his game-keeper's boots, waterproof jacket and deerstalker.

Danny: could be wearing school uniform, or his jeans and T-shirt.

Dad: wearing his overalls with one leg in plaster.

Sergeant Samways: wearing police uniform.

SETTING

If your stage has curtains, they should be closed for the first part of the play. The school scene is played in front of them. Then the curtains are drawn, to reveal the caravan and the petrol pumps.

The cut-out Rolls-Royce would be effective, but is not essential. [See illustration on page 15.]

PROPS

Headteacher's cane.

Dad's plaster cast and crutch.

Sergeant Samways' bicycle.

Letter from the Council, in an envelope.

Cup or mug of tea.

SOUND EFFECTS

The choir could sing unaccompanied. Or a musician could play the piano. Or Mr Jackson could play the guitar.

The choir could make the high-pitched 'sound of pain'. Or this could be an electronic noise made on a keyboard.

Car noises (of the Rolls-Royce) could be recorded, or voiced by the choir.

LIGHTING

A black-out would be highly effective just before Danny is caned. But if this is impossible, the caning could be done in slow motion. Or the Headteacher and Danny could freeze during the 'sound of pain'.

HAZELL COMES TO SCHOOL

Curtain up.

The CHOIR *form part of the audience. The* NARRATOR *enters.*

NARRATOR: Danny's Dad runs a small filling station on the edge of a village. He also poaches pheasants from Hazell's Wood. When he falls into a mantrap, set by Mr Hazell, the local landowner, and breaks his ankle, Danny bravely rescues him. Today Danny has come to school.

CHOIR: [*Singing*] ALL THINGS BRIGHT AND BEAUTIFUL
ALL CREATURES GREAT AND SMALL
ALL THINGS WISE AND WONDERFUL
[*Enter the* HEADTEACHER *and another teacher* (MR JACKSON). *They face the audience. It is school assembly*]

ALL: THE LORD GOD MADE THEM ALL.

HEADTEACHER: This morning, boys and girls, is a special morning. Settle down. No talking. This morning we have two 'visitors' with something very exciting to talk about. So sit up straight, legs crossed, arms folded. Gillian, I'm not telling you again, stop doing that to Brian. [*Nodding to the other teacher*] Thank you, Mr Jackson.

[MR JACKSON *exits to collect the visitors*]

Now, let's give a warm St Wilberforce School welcome to our visitors.

[*She encourages the audience to applaud*]

[MR JACKSON *returns with* HAZELL *and* RABBETTS]

HAZELL: Thank you, Headteacher. Good morning, children. My name is Mr Hazell. Like you I started off from very humble beginnings, but I worked hard and became very successful, brewing beer. You may have noticed me driving in my very expensive Rolls-Royce. Nice, isn't it? Now, this coming Saturday it will be October the first. Anyone know what's so special about October the first? Well, I'll tell you. It's the start of the pheasant-shooting season, and, as is customary, I shall be inviting to Hazell Hall, my country seat, all my distinguished friends, Dukes and Lords, Barons and Baronets, that sort of chap, to what is generally accepted as the best Pheasant Shooting Party in the county – country, more like. And this year, some of you kiddies are invited to join in the fun.

[*The* HEADTEACHER *and* MR JACKSON *react pleased*]

Now, this is Mr Rabbetts, my Head Gamekeeper, and he'll tell you a bit more.

[*He pushes* RABBETTS *forward*]

RABBETTS: Right. Yes, well, what the boss . . . er, Mr Hazell . . . wants is for some of you kids to be beaters. What beaters do is come up to Hazell's Wood, where all the pheasants are, and when all the boss's . . . er, Mr Hazell's posh guests are ready with their shotguns, you start yelling and shouting and bashing away at the undergrowth, to make the pheasants fly up ready to be shot.

HAZELL: Show 'em, Rabbetts. Give 'em a demonstration.

RABBETTS: [*Embarrassed*] Right, sir.
[*He starts yelling and miming the 'beating', stamping on the floor*]

HAZELL: That's enough. So we want some volunteers. Who would like to be a beater? Hands up!
[*Suddenly he is interrupted by a voice from the audience*]

DANNY: No! Do your own dirty work!
[HAZELL *looks up*]

HEADTEACHER: Who said that?

DANNY: Murderer!

HEADTEACHER: Daniel? Sit down and be quiet.

DANNY: No, Miss. It's wrong. Shooting beautiful birds for fun! It's wrong!

HEADTEACHER: Quiet! Mr Jackson!
[MR JACKSON *hurries into the audience to restrain* DANNY]

DANNY: Murderer!

HAZELL: Who is that boy?

HEADTEACHER: Daniel, he . . .

DANNY: They haven't done any harm! Why shoot them? Shoot him instead!
[MR JACKSON *is dragging* DANNY *on to the stage*]

HAZELL: [*Realizing*] The boy from the filling station! I know you.

DANNY: And I know you, Mr Hazell. And I don't like what you do.

HEADTEACHER: Daniel. SHUT UP!
[DANNY *is quiet*]

I'm very sorry, Mr Hazell. I'm quite sure we have many children who will be delighted to be beaters. I'll be in touch.

HAZELL: Very well, Headteacher.
[*He and* RABBETTS *turn to go.* RABBETTS *exits.* HAZELL *turns back*]

And I hope this rude boy won't be allowed to get away with his wild interruption. He must be punished.
[*He exits*]

HEADTEACHER: Daniel, how dare you behave like that when we have visitors.

DANNY: But, Miss . . .

HEADTEACHER: No buts, Daniel. You were very rude.

I quite understand you feel strongly about shooting birds for sport. Many people agree with you it is unacceptable.

DANNY: It's wrong, Miss . . .

HEADTEACHER: But it is not illegal, and you cannot just shout and scream at people like Mr Hazell because you don't agree with them. We live in a community, Daniel. We have to get along. Live and let live. Civilized behaviour. Now, hold out your hand.

[*She produces a cane*]

[DANNY *hesitates*]

Now!

[DANNY *fearfully holds out his hand. The* HEAD-TEACHER *raises the cane. As she goes to strike . . .*]

[*The lights black out*]

CHOIR: [*A high-pitched sound of pain*]

[*The curtains are drawn to reveal the cut-out caravan and the petrol pumps, one each side*]

[*As the* CHOIR *cut out, the lights fade up to reveal* DAD *and* SERGEANT SAMWAYS *with his bicycle*]

DAD: Barbaric it was, Sergeant. They shouldn't be allowed to hit children.

SERGEANT SAMWAYS: Danny all right?

DAD: He's not complaining. But you can still see the mark on his hand. It's not right.

SERGEANT SAMWAYS: I got caned once. Old Hotty Wootton, the teacher, he used to sit on my desk when chatting to the class, you know. So one day I overfilled the inkwell – you remember them inkwells we used to have? He sits down and gets an inky bum! Ha, ha. Then I gets a sore bum!

DAD: Danny wasn't even misbehaving. Just standing up for what he believes.

SERGEANT SAMWAYS: And standing up to Hazell, by the sound of it.

DAD: [*Smiling*] Well, yes.

SERGEANT SAMWAYS: [*Pointing to* DAD*'s plastered leg*] And you've been in the wars too, eh, Willum? In Hazell's Wood?

DAD: Yes.

SERGEANT SAMWAYS: Be careful, Willum. You know what he's like.
   [DAD *nods*]

DAD: And I'm sorry your pride and joy's not serviced yet, what with one thing and another . . .

SERGEANT SAMWAYS: No worry, no hurry, Willum. I'll be back in a day or two. [*Looking off*] Ah, speak of the devil . . . Watch it, Willum.

[*As he cycles off one side, enter, from the other side,* HAZELL *in his Rolls. Car sounds. The car stops.* HAZELL *gets out.* DAD *tries to keep calm*]

HAZELL: [*With a supercilious smile*] Afternoon.
[DAD *nods*]

[*Knowingly looking at* DAD*'s leg*] Had an accident, have we? Or a fall, perhaps?

DAD: Mr Hazell, I thought I made it clear that I have no wish to serve you.

HAZELL: You made it perfectly clear that you have no wish to serve me. But I wish to serve you . . . with this!
[*He throws a letter at* DAD, *climbs back in the Rolls, then drives off laughing. Car sounds*]

[*As* DAD *opens the envelope,* DANNY *comes from the caravan with a cup of tea.* DAD *starts to read*]

DANNY: Tea, Dad?
[DAD *nods an acknowledgement, but reads on, shocked*]

What is it?

DAD: Letter from the Council.
[*He hands it to* DANNY]

DANNY: [*Reading*] 'It has been decided that your caravan is unfit for human habitation.' What does that mean?

DAD: Read the last bit.

DANNY: [*Reading*] 'The Council will compulsorily now confiscate your land and sell it to the highest bidder. Signed, Councillor Clark.' Dad?

DAD: Hazell's won. Four weeks' notice. He's getting rid of us, Danny. We'll have nowhere to live . . .
[*The lighting fades*]

[*Curtain down*]

OPERATION SLEEPING BEAUTY

Danny's brilliant plan and its execution are featured in this play. Danny and Dad have the biggest roles, and there are other opportunities for actors, puppeteers and a musician. A certain amount of invention will be required to arrange for prop pheasants to drop to the ground from above!

CHARACTERS
Dad and Danny: Danny is wearing pyjamas and Dad is dressed in jeans and T-shirt; when they set off for Hazell's Wood, they need another layer of dark clothes – sweaters or donkey jackets. Dad has a plaster cast on one leg.

Rabbetts, Hazell's head gamekeeper: wearing boots and a waterproof coat, plus a cap or deerstalker.

Several Puppeteers: operate pheasant puppets, and should wear dark clothes.

Charlie Kinch, the taxi-driver: wearing ordinary shirt and trousers, with a coat or donkey jacket.

A musician is not essential, but could play effective links between scenes, to suggest the passage of time, and vocally create the sounds of a chicken and a bullfrog.

SETTING

The interior of the caravan should look as cosy as possible, with table and seats, and possibly two bunks. This set should be upstage. Perhaps a set of curtains could screen it off when the scene changes.

The other locations – the road leading to Hazell's Wood, Hazell Wood itself, and the area where Dad and Danny rest – can all be represented simply, in the open space in front of the curtains. This area could have trees at its side.

Pheasants drop, as though from the trees. Ideally they should be released from above the stage, or thrown up from the wings at the side.

PROPS

Dad's plaster cast and walking stick. (A crutch would be too cumbersome for this play.)

A paraffin lamp

A kettle and two mugs.

A jar of raisins, a paper bag, sleeping pills (red capsules) in a bottle, scissors, needle and thread.

A hand-puppet chicken.

Throwing the raisins in Hazell's Wood can be mimed.

Puppet pheasants on rods. These can be operated from offstage or through curtains, or the puppeteers can be seen onstage.

Gamekeeper's shotgun.

Two apples.

Two torches.

Prop pheasants, made like soft toys. At least a dozen!

Two sacks.

SOUND EFFECTS
Chicken clucks.

Bullfrog croaks.

These might best be created vocally by a musician, who could also play linking music between the scenes, to suggest the passage of time. The musician might also use percussion to accompany the falling of the pheasants.

LIGHTING
The interior of the caravan needs to look warm and cosy with light from the paraffin lamp. It is evening.

The journey to Hazell's Wood and the events that take place there should all be in 'moonlight'. But we need to see the actors' faces, so the lighting shouldn't be too dark.

OPERATION SLEEPING BEAUTY

Curtain up.

Early evening. DANNY, *in his pyjamas, is doing his homework.* DAD *pours water from a kettle into two mugs. He wears his plaster cast.*

NARRATOR: Danny and his father have been served an eviction order by the Council. They will have to leave their home. Dad suspects this is the work of Mr Hazell, a local landowner, who wants to acquire the land on which their caravan and filling station stand. The villagers have started a petition, demanding that Danny and his father be allowed to stay. Meanwhile, the day of Mr Hazell's pheasant shoot is approaching.

DAD: [*Handing* DANNY *a mug*] Cocoa.

DANNY: Thanks, Dad.

DAD: Nearly finished your homework?

DANNY: Yes.

DAD: Better get a move on. Be dark soon.
  [*He drinks, deep in thought*]

DANNY: [*After a pause*] It's good about the petition.

DAD: [*Not really hearing*] Mmm.

DANNY: If everybody signs, maybe Mr Hazell will have to back down.

DAD: Maybe.

DANNY: [*Realizing* DAD *is thinking*] Dad.

DAD: What?

DANNY: What are you plotting?

DAD: Me? Plotting?

DANNY: I can tell.

DAD: I'm not!

DANNY: Tell me. No more secrets. You promised.

DAD: [*With a smile*] I was just thinking . . .

DANNY: What?

DAD: I was thinking about Hazell's Shooting Party on October the first.

DANNY: Go on.

DAD: [*Smiling*] Wouldn't it be marvellous to somehow magically find a way of poaching so many pheasants from Hazell's Wood that there wouldn't be any left for the shoot. To somehow knock off a couple of hundred birds all in one go! So Hazell's party would be the biggest wash-out in history! Wouldn't it be terrific? All those posh dukes and lords and local bigwigs arriving in their flash cars. Hazell strutting around like a peacock welcoming them. Then up to the wood with their guns, the beaters beating and yelling . . . and not a single pheasant flies up! What a triumph! What a victory! And Hazell's face redder than a boiled beetroot! Wouldn't it be great!

DANNY: You're not serious.

DAD: No, Danny, of course not. It's hard enough catching *one* pheasant, let alone two hundred. I've got a broken ankle to prove it. But it's a lovely thought. Come on now, bedtime.

DANNY: How *is* your ankle?

DAD: Throbbing a bit.

DANNY: Better lie down. And take a sleeping pill tonight.

DAD: No. Can't be doing with those things. Come on, bed.

DANNY: [*Suddenly*] Dad, suppose . . .

DAD: [*Warning*] Danny . . .

DANNY: No, Dad, listen. I've got an idea. Your sleeping pills. Is there any reason why they wouldn't work on a pheasant?

DAD: No chance, Danny. No pheasant in the world's going to swallow one of those lousy red capsules!

DANNY: But if we opened up the capsules and put the powder in some raisins, maybe . . .

DAD: [*Softly at first*] Oh, my darling boy. Oh, my sainted aunt! I do believe you've got it! I do, I do, I do! [*His mind races as he thinks it through*]

DANNY: You reckon it might work?

DAD: It'll work all right! Put the powder in two hundred raisins, scatter them around the feeding grounds at sunset, then walk away. Then, after it's dark and the keepers have gone home, back into the wood . . . the pheasants would be up in the trees by then, roosting . . . then the pills start to work . . . pheasants start feeling groggy . . . wobbling and trying to keep their balance . . . then they all topple over unconscious and fall to the ground! Dropping out of the trees like apples! And all I'd have to do is go around picking them up!

DANNY: Can I do it with you, Dad?

DAD: And there's no chance of being caught! Just stroll through the woods dropping a few raisins here and there. The keepers wouldn't notice a thing!

DANNY: Will you let me come too, Dad?

DAD: Danny, my love, if this thing works, it'll revolutionize poaching!

DANNY: Yes, Dad, but can I come with you?

DAD: Come with me?
[*A moment of uncertainty for* DANNY]

My dear boy, of course you can come with me! It's your idea! You must be there to see it happening! Now then, where are those pills?

DANNY: Shouldn't we try it out?

DAD: How?

DANNY: Like your dad used to!

DAD and DANNY: [*Together*] Chicken!
[DANNY *dashes outside the caravan, while* DAD *brings the sleeping pills, the raisins and a pair of scissors to the table.* DANNY *returns with a chicken, which clucks*]

DAD: [*As he carefully divides a capsule, then puts some powder in a raisin*] There are fifty capsules, so if we divide the powder from each one among four raisins, we can get two hundred.

DANNY: Will that be enough powder to send the pheasants to sleep?

DAD: Of course! A pheasant's much smaller than a man!
[*He has prepared a raisin. He holds it in the outstretched palm of his hand*]

Now, chick chick, here's a tasty titbit for you.
[*The chicken examines it*]

DANNY: Go on, it's scrummy!
[*The chicken suddenly pecks at it and swallows it*]

DAD and DANNY: [*Together*] Yeees!
[*The chicken is still animated*]

DANNY: Doesn't look too sleepy.

DAD: Give her time! Give her time!
[*They watch the chicken*]

DANNY: [*A thought*] Dad.

DAD: Yes?

DANNY: Two hundred raisins aren't going to get you two hundred pheasants.

DAD: Why not?

DANNY: Because surely the greediest birds will gobble up about ten raisins each.

DAD: You've got a point there. But somehow I don't think it'll happen that way. Not if I'm very careful and spread them out over a wide area.

DANNY: And you promise I can come with you?

DAD: Absolutely. And we shall call this method The Sleeping Beauty. It will be a landmark in the history of poaching! Exciting, isn't it?

DANNY: Mmm. Bit scary too.

DAD: No time to be scared. We've got to make our plans. The Shooting Party's on October the first.

DANNY: Saturday. When do we do the job?

DAD: Friday. We've got two days to get ready. And Danny . . .

DANNY: Yes?

DAD: Not a whisper of this to any of your friends at school.

DANNY: Course not. Hey, Dad, look!

DAD: What?
[DANNY *indicates the chicken. It is asleep. They both smile, delighted*]

DAD and DANNY: [*Together*] The Sleeping Beauty!
[DANNY *grabs some dark clothes and steps outside the caravan to talk to the audience. Meanwhile* DAD *sets to work on the raisins inside. Two days have passed. The lighting darkens slightly*]

DANNY: [*Putting on his clothes over his pyjamas*] Tonight's the night! We've been working really hard. Dad even let me take the day off school to make sure we got the raisins ready in time. It's really fiddly, opening the capsules, dividing the powder, cutting a slit in the raisins, putting the powder in, then sewing them up.
[DANNY, *dressed, goes inside the caravan.* DAD *is finishing off the preparations, using a needle and thread*]

DAD: Your mum was wonderful at sewing things. She'd have had these raisins done in no time. Made all my clothes, you know, Danny.

DANNY: Even socks and sweaters?

DAD: Yes. Great knitter. She'd sit here, needles flying in her fingers so fast you couldn't see them. I used to watch her and she used to say, 'We'll have three children. A boy for you, a girl for me, and one for good measure.'

[*He pauses.* DANNY *senses* DAD*'s continuing grief*]

DANNY: When Mum was here, Dad, did you go out poaching?

DAD: [*Smiling*] Yes. At least twice a week.

DANNY: Didn't she mind?

DAD: Mind? Of course she didn't mind. She came with me!

DANNY: She didn't!

DAD: She certainly did. Every single time until just before you were born. She had to stop then. She said she couldn't run fast enough!

DANNY: Did she come with you just because she loved you, Dad? Or because she loved poaching?

DAD: [*Proudly*] Both, Danny, both. She was a great sport, your mother. [*Finishing the last raisin*] Right. All done. Let's go. Operation Sleeping Beauty!

[DAD *and* DANNY *finish dressing for the trip, collect the raisins in a paper bag and leave the caravan. Then they begin to walk down the road to Hazell's Wood, as the curtains close, hiding the caravan*]

[*After a pause . . .* DANNY *is somewhat nervous*]

DAD: [*Bright*] How do you feel, Danny?

DANNY: Terrific. [*After a pause*] Do you think they might've dug any more of those pits?

DAD: We'll keep a good look-out, don't you worry.
[*The sound of a bullfrog croaking*]

Do you hear that?
[*They stop. Another croak*]

DANNY: Yes.

DAD: It's a bullfrog calling to his wife. He does it by blowing out his dewlap and letting it go with a burp.

DANNY: What's a dewlap?

DAD: The loose skin on his throat. He can blow it up just like a little balloon.
[*Another croak*]

DANNY: What happens when his wife hears him?

DAD: She goes hopping over to him, happy to be invited. But often he's so pleased with the sound of his own voice that his wife has to nudge him a few times before he'll stop his burping and give her a hug!
[DANNY *laughs. Another croak*]

We men aren't so different from the bullfrog, I reckon.
[*Another croak. They walk a few paces*]

Wild animals teach us lots about ourselves, you know.

DANNY: Pheasants aren't really wild, are they?

DAD: Course they are.

DANNY: But not Mr Hazell's pheasants. You said he buys them as chicks and feeds them. Like pets almost.

DAD: Ah yes. But the law says they're wild birds. They only belong to you when they're on your own land. Even if you've paid for them.

DANNY: Really?

DAD: Like trout. If a trout swims out of your stretch of water into someone else's you can't say, 'Hey, that's mine. I want it back.'

DANNY: So, say if one of Mr Hazell's pheasants flew away and landed on the filling station . . .

DAD: It would belong to us.

DANNY: Really?

DAD: Yes. Till it flew back again! Come on, this way.
[DAD *and* DANNY *change direction and arrive in Hazell's Wood.* DAD *takes* DANNY*'s hand as they creep carefully into the wood, trying not to make a sound*]

[*Suddenly they see something.* DAD *gestures to* DANNY *and they both throw themselves to the ground and lie still*]

[RABBETTS *enters, walks a few paces towards them, then turns and exits*]

[DAD *and* DANNY *crawl on hands and knees. They reach the edge of the clearing, where suddenly they see pheasants strutting about.* DAD *points them out to* DANNY. *They watch in delighted anticipation*]

[*Suddenly* RABBETTS *appears again.* DAD *pushes* DANNY *down, then flattens himself.* RABBETTS *strolls across and exits*]

[DAD *carefully takes out the bag of raisins. He throws one into the clearing, then another. Small flurries of movement as pheasants find them and eat them.* DAD *throws a few more, further away. More pheasants react and eat*]

[*Suddenly* RABBETTS *appears again.* DAD *and* DANNY *react, keeping low. This time* RABBETTS *stays in view, looking in the other direction.* DAD *carefully throws more raisins. The pheasants react. Then* DAD *takes the whole bag, and, in spite of* DANNY*'s worried look, throws a huge handful of raisins into the clearing*]

[*The pheasants react with a loud flurry of movement as they rush to find the raisins.* RABBETTS*'s head springs round as he hears the sound. He cocks his gun.* DAD *and* DANNY *duck down again.* RABBETTS *seems to be suspicious. He walks forward and surveys the scene, then turns, with his back to* DAD *and* DANNY]

[DAD *motions to* DANNY *to follow. They crawl away on their hands and knees and exit.* RABBETTS *uncocks his gun as he takes another look, then exits, in the other direction*]

[*After a pause,* DAD *and* DANNY *enter breathless. They sit down*]

DAD: We did it, Danny! We pulled it off! Doesn't that make you feel good?

DANNY: Terrific. Scary, though.

DAD: Ah, but that's what poaching's all about! It scares the pants off us. That's why we love it! [*Producing apples from his pocket*] Cox's Orange Pippin?

DANNY: [*Taking one*] Thanks.

DAD: Shake it.
[*They both shake their apples*]

Can you hear the pips rattling?

DANNY: Yes.

DAD: That means it's ripe!
[*They take a bite out of their apples*]

[*Enter* RABBETTS. DAD *sees him*]

DAD: [*Urgently*] Look out. Sit tight and don't say a word.
[*He takes another bite of apple and puts on an unconcerned expression*]

[RABBETTS *approaches. He stops and looks down at* DAD *and* DANNY]

[*Overtly friendly*] Good evening.

RABBETTS: [*Unsmiling*] I know you. I know the both of you.

    [*Pause.* DAD *eats his apple*]

You're from the fillin' station. Right? And that's your boy, what give us all that lip at the school. Right? And you live in that filthy old caravan. Right?

DAD: Questions, questions. Is this a quiz?

    [RABBETTS *spits. It lands near* DAD*'s foot*]

Charming.

RABBETTS: Beat it. Go on. Get out.

DAD: This happens to be a public footpath. Kindly do not molest us.

    [RABBETTS *shifts his gun from one arm to the other, threateningly*]

RABBETTS: You're loiterin'. With intent to commit a nuisance. I could run you in for that.

    [DANNY *looks nervous*]

DAD: No, you couldn't. We're just having a rest before walking home.

RABBETTS: I see you broke your foot. You didn't by any chance fall into a hole in the ground, did you?

DAD: Why don't you leave us alone? We're doing no harm.

RABBETTS: You watch it. Or I'll break the other foot for you.

[*He sniffs, then walks away and exits*]

DANNY: He's called Rabbetts.

DAD: Mmm. Nasty bit of work.

DANNY: Will he come back?

DAD: Doubt it. Gone home for his tea. Don't worry about him. Come on, Danny. It's getting dark. We're going back!
[*They get up and start walking, returning to Hazell's Wood. They take out torches and turn them on*]

[DAD *and* DANNY *arrive. There is no sign of any pheasants.* DAD *and* DANNY *shine their torches. They speak in whispers*]

DANNY: Are they all roosting, Dad?

DAD: Yes. High up in the branches.
[*They turn off their torches*]

This will be the first time in the world that anyone has tried to poach roosting pheasants! And it's all thanks to you, Danny. Now let's wait for them to fall like raindrops from the sky.
[*Pause*]

DANNY: Dad.

DAD: Yes?

DANNY: When birds roost in trees, they go to sleep, right?

DAD: Right.

DANNY: So why don't they topple off the branches? *We* would if we tried to sleep up there.

DAD: Birds have claws and long toes. They hold on with those.

DANNY: So why should the sleeping powder make them fall down?
[*Pause*]

DAD: Well, it makes them sleep deeper.

DANNY: But if they're holding on with their claws . . .

DAD: You might be right.

DANNY: In which case, my idea won't . . .
[DAD *and* DANNY *look at each other, momentarily discouraged*]

[*But then . . . a soft thump is heard as a pheasant falls; and another; and another*]

[*Shining his torch*] Look, Dad! It's working!

DAD: Beautiful! It's beautiful!
[*More and more thumps as more and more pheasants fall*]

Yes! Yes!

DANNY: It's raining pheasants!
[DAD *and* DANNY *step into the centre as pheasants rain down around them*]

DAD: It's a triumph!
[*He takes out two sacks from under his coat and hands one to* DANNY. *They start picking up the pheasants and filling the sacks*]

What would Mr Victor Hazell think if he could see this?

DANNY: Don't think about it, Dad!

DAD: I can't help it, Danny! It's just what I wanted! It's a miracle!
[*Suddenly, as they continue stuffing the sacks, a voice rings out*]

VOICE OFFSTAGE: Hello, hello, hello! What's all this then?
[DAD *and* DANNY *freeze*]

[*Somebody enters the clearing*]

VOICE: Just as I thought! Caught red-handed!
[DAD *and* DANNY *look round*]

Ha, ha, ha! Got you! Fooled you!
[*It is* CHARLIE]

DAD: Charlie! Thank heavens it's you. It's all right, Danny. It's Charlie.

DANNY: Mr Kinch! What are you doing here?

CHARLIE: Brought the taxi, just like I said I would! You need it by the look of things!

DAD: Sorry, Danny. I forgot to tell you.

DANNY: Another secret, Dad?

DAD: Not really. But I knew we couldn't carry this lot on our own!
[CHARLIE *helps them stuff the remaining pheasants in the sacks*]

DANNY: So you knew about Dad's poaching, Mr Kinch?

CHARLIE: Course, Danny. I've poached more pheasants in my time than you've sold gallons of petrol! But never as many as this in one go! I reckon as this is a record! Come on! The taxi's over there.

DAD: And it's all thanks to Danny, Charlie. He's Champion of the Village!

CHARLIE: He is indeed [*Announcing*] Danny . . . *

DAD and CHARLIE: The Champion of the Village!
[*They all drag the sacks offstage towards the taxi*]

[*Curtain down*]

* *If you are only performing this play, and not the concluding one, 'The Shooting Party', as well, you might like to try this alternative ending:*

CHARLIE: Of the Village? Of the World!

DAD: You're right, Charlie. [*Announcing*] Danny . . .

DAD and CHARLIE: The Champion of the World!
   [*They all drag the sacks offstage towards the taxi*]

[*Curtain down*]

HACCUSATIONS

The comic and the serious work side by side in this play. There are six strong acting roles plus opportunities for several puppeteers, who operate the pheasant puppets, around which the play revolves.

CHARACTERS
Narrator

Danny: wearing jeans and a T-shirt.

Doctor Spencer: wearing country tweeds.

Dad: wearing overalls and a plaster cast on one leg.

Mrs Clipstone: wearing a sensible skirt and top.

Hazell: wearing his smart, if somewhat vulgar, Shooting Party tweeds.

Sergeant Samways: wearing his police uniform.

Several Puppeteers: operate pheasant puppets, and should wear dark clothes.

SETTING
Upstage centre is the caravan exterior. The puppeteers need room behind it.

Downstage each side is a cut-out petrol pump.

There must be room for the cut-out Rolls-Royce (Hazell's car) to enter part-way. [See illustration on page 15.]

PROPS
Dad's plaster cast and walking stick.

A 'Sorry, closed' notice that hangs round a petrol pump.

Doctor's bag.

Oily rag.

Petition forms.

Old-fashioned pram, with a doll representing the baby.

Puppet pheasants. These should be on rods, four of them in pairs or in fours – 'sprays' of birds. The puppeteers can make them appear to fly from the pram, and also fly in from offstage, then land on the caravan roof, the petrol pumps and the roof of the Rolls. It may be easier for those landing on the bonnet of the Rolls to be on shorter rods, or even to be hand puppets, manipulated from behind.

Sergeant Samways could enter on a bicycle, but this is not essential.

A whistle for Sergeant Samways.

Eviction order.

SOUND EFFECTS
Noise from the workshop offstage – banging, etc.

The sound of the baby screaming.

The arrival and departure of the Rolls.

These effects could be created with percussion and vocally. Or they could be recorded.

LIGHTING
No special lighting is required. It can be bright throughout. But it might be fun to flicker the lights when the pheasants are 'flying'.

HACCUSATIONS

Curtain up.

NARRATOR: Danny has invented a brand-new method of poaching pheasants – 'The Sleeping Beauty'. He and his Dad insert sleeping powder in raisins, which the pheasants eat. They fall into a deep sleep and drop from their roosts in the trees. Dad and Danny deliver them to Mrs Clipstone, the vicar's wife, for safe keeping. The pheasants were being prepared for the unpleasant landowner Mr Hazell and his Shooting Party guests to shoot. Earlier, thanks to Hazell, Dad and Danny were served an eviction order, meaning they will soon have to leave their caravan home and their filling station.

> [*Noise of activity in the workshop.* DANNY *enters and removes the 'Sorry, closed' notice as* DOCTOR SPENCER *enters, carrying a doctor's bag*]

DOCTOR SPENCER: Danny! Good morning!

DANNY: Morning, Doctor Spencer.

DOCTOR SPENCER: [*Warmly shaking* DANNY*'s hand*] Congratulations, my dear, well done!

DANNY: Eh?

DOCTOR SPENCER: The Sleeping Beauty! Brilliant! Your dad rang me with the splendid news! A brilliant idea! Why didn't I think of it myself?

DANNY: Well, it was thanks to your sleeping pills.

DOCTOR SPENCER: You're a genius, Danny!

DAD: [*Emerging from the workshop, wiping his oily hands*] Too right, Doc. I told him he's Champion of the Village!

DOCTOR SPENCER: Of the Village? He's Champion of the County. Hail to thee, Champion Danny!
[DANNY *laughs*]

Now, William, look.
[DOCTOR SPENCER *brings out the petition forms from the bag*]

DAD: What's that?

DOCTOR SPENCER: The petition, William, the petition. Everyone's signed, some people twice! I'll deliver it to the Council and hope they see sense.

DAD: [*Looking at it*] Well, thank you, Doc. It's great to know we've got so much support. Eh, Danny?

DANNY: Great. [*Seeing something offstage*] Look, Dad. It's Mrs Clipstone, with Christopher.

DAD: [*Looking at his watch*] Excellent! Bang on time! What a woman! This is her sixth delivery this morning!

DOCTOR SPENCER: How do you mean?

DAD: There's only one way of delivering pheasants safely.

DANNY: And that's under a baby.

DOCTOR SPENCER: Under a baby?

DAD: In a pram.

DANNY: With the baby on top!

DOCTOR SPENCER: What a brilliant idea!

DANNY: Right through the village!

DAD: Bold as brass!

DOCTOR SPENCER: Good for her!

DAD: We're storing the pheasants in the workshop.

DANNY: Why's she running, Dad?
   [*The sound of a baby screaming*]

DOCTOR SPENCER: And why's Christopher yelling his
   head off?

DAD: Maybe he's having a fit? Just as well we've got a
   doctor handy.

DANNY: Dad, it might be serious.

DAD: It will be if she gives the game away. Stop running,
   Mrs Clipstone!
   [*Suddenly* MRS CLIPSTONE *enters on the run, pushing
   the pram, the baby screaming*]

MRS CLIPSTONE: Help! Help!

DAD: What is it?

MRS CLIPSTONE: They're pecking him to pieces! Christopher!
[*She lifts the baby out and runs to safety as* DAD *and* DOCTOR SPENCER *look in the pram*]

DOCTOR SPENCER: Great Scott! The sleeping pills are wearing off!

DAD: Look out! They've woken up!
[*Puppeteers enter and make the puppet pheasants appear to fly up and out of the pram. Chaos as they rise, flapping, and land on the caravan and the pumps*]

[DOCTOR SPENCER *checks the baby as* DANNY *takes cover with* MRS CLIPSTONE]

[*Suddenly more pheasants fly from offstage*]

DANNY: They're coming out of the workshop now!
[*More flurry as the pheasants land on the pumps and the caravan. At last they are all settled*]

DAD: [*Emerging from behind the pram*] Best-laid plans . . .
[*He starts to laugh. Everyone joins in*]

Are you all right, Mrs Clipstone?

MRS CLIPSTONE: It's Christopher I'm worried about.

DOCTOR SPENCER: He's fine. No damage done! Eh, Christopher?

DANNY: He's never sat on an exploding mattress before!
[*Everyone is laughing, as a release from the shock*]

DAD: I should have thought. Sleeping pills always wear off by next morning.
[*Suddenly the atmosphere changes as* HAZELL *arrives in his Rolls. He parks to one side. Seeing the pheasants, he gets out of the car, seething with fury*]

HAZELL: [*Apoplectic*] H-h-h-h d-d-d-d y-y-y-y st-st-st-st m-m-m-m ph-ph-ph-ph . . . [*He is trying to say 'How dare you steal my pheasants!'*]
[*He looks madly from pheasants to* DAD, *eyes popping and lips foaming*]

[*Trying to say, 'You'll pay for this!'*] Y-y-y-y p-p-p-p f-f-f-f th-th-th-th . . . [*At last*] m-m-my ph-ph-pheasants! MY PHEASANTS!

DAD: [*Appearing to stay calm*] But they are *not* your pheasants. They're mine.

HAZELL: Don't lie to me, man! I'm the only person around here who has pheasants!

DAD: They are on my land. They flew on to my land, and so long as they stay on my land they belong to me. Don't you know the rules, you bloated old blue-faced baboon?

HAZELL: How dare you!

DAD: How dare *you*!
[*They square up to each other. They talk over each other*]

HAZELL: You're a thief. I've never liked your attitude and I'm pretty sure it was you who we caught in Hazell's Wood the other day, and you won't get away with this [*etc.*]

DAD: Why don't you just drive off in your fancy car and leave us alone? You've always disliked us and been rude and nasty, and these pheasants are *mine* [*etc.*]

[DOCTOR SPENCER *steps between them*]

DOCTOR SPENCER: Mr Hazell, please calm down, and William, come on, let's discuss this in a sensible way [*etc.*]

[DANNY *and* MRS CLIPSTONE *watch.* MRS CLIPSTONE *shields* CHRISTOPHER *from the noisy scene*]

[*As the row continues, enter* SERGEANT SAMWAYS *blowing his whistle. Immediately all fall silent*]

SERGEANT SAMWAYS: [*Adopting his formal policeman persona*] Well, well, well. What, may I hask, is 'appening around 'ere?

HAZELL: I'll tell you what's happening around here. These are my pheasants, and this rogue has enticed them out of my woods on to his filthy little filling station!

SERGEANT SAMWAYS: [*Surveying the scene*] Hen-ticed? Hen-ticed them, did you say?

HAZELL: Of course he enticed them.

SERGEANT SAMWAYS: Well now, this is a very hinterestin' haccusation, very hinterestin' indeed, because I ain't never 'eard of nobody hen-ticin' a pheasant across six miles of fields and open countryside. 'Ow do you think this hen-ticin' was performed, Mr 'Azell, if I may hask?

HAZELL: Don't ask me how he did it because I don't know, but he's done it all right! The proof is all around you! All my finest birds are sitting here in this dirty little filling station when they ought to be up in my own wood getting ready for the shoot!

SERGEANT SAMWAYS: Am I correct, am I habsolutely haccurate in thinkin' that today is the day of your great Shootin' Party, Mr 'Azell?

HAZELL: That's the whole point! [*Prodding* SERGEANT SAMWAYS *with his finger*] And if I don't get these birds back on my land quick sharp, some very important people are going to be extremely angry. One of my guests, I'll have you know, Sergeant, is none other than your own boss, the Chief Constable of the County! So you had better do something about it fast, hadn't you, unless you want to lose those sergeant's stripes of yours.

SERGEANT SAMWAYS: Now just one minute, please. Am I to understand that you are haccusin' this gentleman here of committin' this hact?

HAZELL: Of course I am! I know he did it!

SERGEANT SAMWAYS: And do you 'ave any hevidence to support this haccusation?

HAZELL: The evidence is all around you! Are you blind or something?

[SERGEANT SAMWAYS *bristles*. DAD *steps forward*]

DAD: [*Politely*] Surely you know how these pheasants came here?

HAZELL: Surely I do *not* know.

DAD: Then I shall tell you. Because it is quite simple really.

[DANNY, MRS CLIPSTONE *and* DOCTOR SPENCER *look concerned. Is* DAD *going to admit the truth?*]

They all knew they were going to be shot today if they stayed in your wood, so they flew in here to wait until the shooting was over.

HAZELL: Rubbish!

DAD: It's not rubbish at all. They are extremely intelligent birds, pheasants. Isn't that so, Doctor?

DOCTOR SPENCER: They have tremendous brain-power. They know exactly what's going on.

HAZELL: Balderdash! It's a conspiracy!

DAD: It would undoubtedly be a great honour to be shot by the Chief Constable, and an even greater one to be eaten afterwards by Lord Thistlewaite, but I don't think a pheasant would see it that way.

HAZELL: You are scoundrels, both of you! Rapscallions! Sergeant, the Council has issued a four-week eviction order on this thief and his brat of a son. I order you to kick them out right *now*!

MRS CLIPSTONE: [*Dashing forward*] You can't do that! What about the petition?

DOCTOR SPENCER: Yes, indeed! [*Producing the petition*] All the villagers have signed it, and nothing can happen till the Council considers it.
     [HAZELL *grabs the petition. He looks at it, then ferociously tears it up and throws it to the ground*]

[*All the adults start shouting together*]

HAZELL: That's what I think of your pathetic petition . . .

MRS CLIPSTONE: That's not fair! You can't do that . . .

DOCTOR SPENCER: What on earth do you think you're doing?

DAD: Why don't you just leave us alone?

SERGEANT SAMWAYS: I don't think you should've done that, Mr 'Azell . . .

     [*Suddenly* DANNY *intervenes*]

DANNY: Quiet! Stop it! Please!
[*All, surprised, stop and listen*]

All this shouting and arguing. It won't get us anywhere. It's just silly.

HAZELL: [*About to explode*] What?

DANNY: Please, Mr Hazell, listen. You want the
pheasants for your Shooting Party. Dad and I don't
want to lose our home. Right? [*To the others*] I suggest
we all do our best to drive the pheasants back on to
Mr Hazell's land. And, in return, Mr Hazell, please
will you let us stay here?

HAZELL: [*After a pause*] It's nothing to do with me.

DANNY: I think it is, Mr Hazell. The Council will listen
to you.

HAZELL: Well, I . . .

DAD: [*Producing the eviction order*] You could tear up the
eviction order for a start.

SERGEANT SAMWAYS: Sounds fair to me.

DOCTOR SPENCER: An excellent compromise.

DANNY: Please, Mr Hazell.

HAZELL: [*After a pause*] Oh, very well.

DANNY: [*Racing into action*] Right! Come on, everyone!
Shoo! Shoo!

[*He starts shooing the pheasants.* HAZELL *watches as a frenzy of activity begins. Everyone starts trying to dislodge the pheasants and shoo them away*]

ALL [*except* HAZELL]: Shoo! Off you go! Beat it! Shoo! Get out of here!

[*They create a noise, clapping and hollering, dashing around, arms waving, encouraging the pheasants to leave*]

Come on! Shoo! Scarper! Vamoose!

[*Suddenly all the pheasants lift off in a flock, hover above, then plummet down on to* HAZELL*'s Rolls, covering the roof and the bonnet*]

HAZELL: Not on my car, you idiots! They'll ruin the paintwork!

[*The others can't help smiling at* HAZELL*'s discomfort. They try unsuccessfully to shift the pheasants*]

ALL [*except* HAZELL]: Shoo! Shoo! Go on! Up! Up! [*etc.*]

[*Eventually . . .*]

SERGEANT SAMWAYS: Sorry, Mr 'Azell, we've done our very best to hencourage these birds up and away, but they're too hignorant to hunderstand.

HAZELL: They're on my car!

SERGEANT SAMWAYS: At least they're back on your property, sir. That's a fair result. I'd get in and drive 'er away quick!

[HAZELL *moves towards the car.* DANNY *grabs the eviction order from* DAD]

DANNY: Don't forget to tear this up, Mr Hazell. You promised.

[*He holds out the eviction order to* HAZELL, *who grabs it*]

HAZELL: If you think I'm going to tear this up now, think again! The eviction order stands.

[*He gets in the car and drives off, with the pheasants still covering the car. The others watch, gasping with frustration*]

[*Curtain down*]

THE SHOOTING PARTY

This play concludes the story. It concerns the come-uppance of Hazell and the triumph (at least for now) of Danny and his Dad. Danny's sense of justice and diplomacy skills prove more effective than those of the adults. The play is different from the others in that the audience become characters and help overcome Hazell.

CHARACTERS
Narrator

Hazell: wearing his Shooting Party gear.

The audience: dressed as they come!

Danny: wearing jeans and T-shirt.

Rabbetts: wearing boots and coat.

The Shooting Party: Sir Godfrey
                        Lord Thistlewaite
                        Lady Thistlewaite
                        Councillor Clark

These four have speaking roles. There could be more non-speaking members of the Shooting Party. All are dressed in smart shooting outfits.

Dad: wearing jeans and sweater. One leg is in a plaster cast.

Mrs Clipstone: wearing skirt and top.

Charlie Kinch: wearing his taxi-driver's jacket and trousers.

Doctor Spencer: dressed smartly.

Sergeant Samways: wearing his police uniform.

Several Puppeteers: operate pheasant puppets, and should wear dark clothes.

SETTING
This play can be performed with no set whatsoever! An open space. It could be performed in the round. If scenery is required it should be trees.

PROPS
Dad's plaster cast and walking stick.

Shotguns for Hazell, Rabbetts and the Shooting Party.

Rod-puppet pheasants.

Mrs Clipstone's pram, with doll for the baby.

Eviction order.

Ten prop pheasants (concealed in the pram, under the baby).

SOUND EFFECTS
No sound effects are required.

LIGHTING
No special lighting is required.

THE SHOOTING PARTY

Curtain up.

NARRATOR: Mr Hazell is trying to have Danny and his Dad evicted from their caravan and filling station, even though the villagers have organized a petition to allow them to stay. Earlier, Danny invented 'The Sleeping Beauty', a brilliant method of poaching pheasants. Today is the day of Mr Hazell's Shooting Party. Danny and his Dad disapprove of shooting pheasants for sport.

> [HAZELL *enters and suddenly sees the audience*]

HAZELL: Aha! The beaters have arrived! Splendid! [*With oily and patronizing bonhomie*] Welcome, kiddies. I'm sure you're going to have a jolly time. This will be a day you'll never forget. Now, before we take you up into Hazell's Wood, we're going to give you a practice in the finer skills of beating. [*He looks around*] Rabbetts? Where are you, man? [*To the audience*] Excuse me. Stay there. [*Calling*] Rabbetts!

> [*He exits in search*]

> [DANNY *quickly enters*]

DANNY: [*Urgently to the audience*] Hey, listen, everyone. I've had an idea. I don't think any of us really want this Shooting Party to go ahead, do we? Eh?

> [*Hopefully the audience agree*]

Well, listen, if we all go along with this beating practice, if we pretend to be on Hazell's side, I'm sure we can stop the Shooting Party happening. OK? Trust me! You see, what we'll do . . .

[*He looks off and sees* HAZELL *and* RABBETTS *returning*]

He's coming back! Please! Pretend you're on his side!

[*He speedily exits or becomes one of the audience*]

[*Enter* HAZELL *and* RABBETTS]

HAZELL: [*To the audience*] Right. Beater training. So, beaters, first of all, please stand up! Come on. Everybody up.

[*The audience stand*]

Splendid. Rabbetts, over to you.

RABBETTS: Right, boss. [*To the audience*] Now your job is to scare the birds to make 'em fly up. So first, please stamp your feet. Go on! Stamp, stamp, stamp!

[*He demonstrates and the audience join in*]

Yes. Good! Good!

HAZELL: Next you make a whooping noise. [*Thinking how to describe it*] Like a police-car siren.

[*He demonstrates*]

Whoo, whoo, whoo, whoo! Everybody!

AUDIENCE: Whoo, whoo, whoo, whoo!

HAZELL: Yes! You've got it! Excellent.

RABBETTS: And then you clap. Hard, like this!
[*He claps quickly, several times*]

Everyone!
[*The audience clap*]

RABBETTS: Thank you. That'll work a treat.

HAZELL: Well done! Well done! Now, let's put it all together. Here we go. Rabbetts!

RABBETTS: Stamp!
[*He leads the stamping*]

HAZELL: Whoo!
[*He leads the siren noise*]

RABBETTS: Clap!
[*He leads the clapping*]

HAZELL: [*Quietening the audience*] Perfect! Outstanding! Thank you. Sit down again, please. We'll see you in the wood. Come on, Rabbetts, time to meet our guests.
[*They exit*]

[DANNY *returns*]

DANNY: [*To the audience*] Great! Thank you. Now, listen. Here's the plan. We all go to Hazell's Wood and get there before the Shooting Party. Then we start beating early, so all the pheasants fly up and escape before the shooting starts. So everyone, very quiet until . . .

[*He sees* HAZELL *approaching, and hides in the audience*]

[HAZELL *enters, leading the Shooting Party. All carry shotguns*]

HAZELL: [*Unctuously*] My dear Sir Godfrey, Lady Thistlewaite, Lord Thistlewaite, Councillor Clark, you are most welcome! This is a great season for pheasants, a very great season indeed! Please, follow me, there are drinks this way. A glass of chilled champagne? Or some mulled wine, perhaps? This way, please!

[*He leads them off*]

[DANNY *returns*]

[*Pheasants enter and strut about*]

DANNY: [*Whispering to the audience*] Here we are! This is it! Everybody, please, quietly stand up!

[*The audience stand*]

Ready! Steady! Beat!

[*He leads the audience. Stamping, whooping and clapping*]

[*The pheasants all react. They fly up, off and away*]

We did it! Yeah!

[*He leads the audience, cheering*]

[*Suddenly he sees the Shooting Party approaching*]

They're coming! Shh! Stay standing! Shh! Good luck!

[*He joins the audience*]

[*Enter* HAZELL *and* RABBETTS, *leading the Shooting Party. They all gather*]

HAZELL: My lords, ladies and gentlemen. The moment we have all waited for has arrived. Please prepare your shotguns.
[*The Shooting Party cock their shotguns in readiness*]

Good sport, everybody. Rabbetts!
[RABBETTS *steps forward*]

RABBETTS: [*To the audience*] Beaters stand by! Beaters, BEAT!
[*He leads the audience. Stamps. Whoops. Claps*]

[*Nothing happens. The Shooting Party silently aim, but no birds fly up*]

HAZELL: [*Whispers*] Rabbetts, what's going on?

RABBETTS: Nothing, sir. Don't understand it.

HAZELL: Again!

RABBETTS: Beaters, BEAT!
[*He leads the audience again. Stamps. Whoops. Claps*]

[*Nothing happens*]

[*The Shooting Party members relax their aim. They turn to* HAZELL]

SIR GODFREY: What's all this, Hazell? Where are the pheasants?

HAZELL: Sir Godfrey, please . . .

LORD THISTLEWAITE: Sheer waste of time! Not a single bird!

HAZELL: Lord Thistlewaite, I'm sure . . .

LADY THISTLEWAITE: Absolute wash-out! Time to go!

HAZELL: Lady Thistlewaite, let's try again . . .

COUNCILLOR CLARK: Disgraceful! I've had enough.

HAZELL: Councillor Clark, no, don't go, please! [*To all*] Stay for another glass of champagne!
  [*The guests start to exit, muttering*]

SIR GODFREY: Never liked the man!

LORD THISTLEWAITE: Jumped-up little upstart!

LADY THISTLEWAITE: Won't bother to come again!

COUNCILLOR CLARK: What a shambles!
  [HAZELL *is left alone, humbled. He turns on* RABBETTS]

HAZELL: Rabbetts!

RABBETTS: [*Hurriedly exiting*] Sorry, boss. Nothing to do with me, boss.
  [HAZELL *turns his attention to the audience*]

HAZELL: [*Realizing the truth*] It was YOU! How dare you sabotage my Shooting Party! How dare you make me a laughing-stock! It's not funny!
  [*Hopefully the audience starts to laugh*]

It's not funny! Shut up!
[*He shakes his fists*]

[DANNY *appears*]

DANNY: It wasn't their fault, Mr Hazell. [*To the audience*] Sit down, everyone, please. [*To* HAZELL] It wasn't their fault. It was my idea to do the beating early.

HAZELL: I might have guessed. Like father like son. Trouble.

DANNY: I didn't want those pheasants shot, in cold blood, just for fun. Maybe I shouldn't have helped them escape and maybe Dad shouldn't go poaching on your land, though it's gone on for years and doesn't really do much harm. All right, we were wrong. But not as wrong as you, Mr Hazell, just because you're rich, thinking you can do as you please, dig pits to catch people in, send spies to look at the caravan and get the Council to try and throw Dad and me out of our home. That's wrong. Just because you want to own *all* the land, you try to get your hands on ours. That's not fair. You're a bully, Mr Hazell, and I don't see why you should get away with it.

[*As he speaks,* DAD, MRS CLIPSTONE *with her pram,* CHARLIE *and* DOCTOR SPENCER *silently enter and stand protectively behind him*]

My dad's worth a hundred of you, Mr Hazell. He's kind. He helps people. He's looked after me since I was a baby. The village like him. And they don't like you. Cos you think you're special. Not one of us. Why can't you live and let live? [*Pause*] Let us stay here . . . please?

[HAZELL *stands motionless*]

DAD: Well said, Danny.

CHARLIE: We're right behind you, lad.

MRS CLIPSTONE: The whole village is behind you, Danny.

DOCTOR SPENCER: Well, Mr Hazell?

[HAZELL *thinks, then pulls out the eviction order*]

HAZELL: It's quite clear. That filling station, that caravan, they don't meet the regulations. It's the law! There's nothing I can do.

DOCTOR SPENCER: What regulations?

HAZELL: It's in black and white, I tell you. [*Reading from the eviction order*] No electricity in the caravan. No running water. Unhygienic chickens running loose. It's quite clear. Unfit for human habitation. Four weeks' notice.

MRS CLIPSTONE: There's electricity in your workshop, isn't there, William?

DAD: Of course. Couldn't fix the cars without it.

DANNY: [*Idea*] Couldn't we wire up the caravan from the workshop?

MRS CLIPSTONE: I'm sure the Electricity Board could easily do that.

DOCTOR SPENCER: And there's water by the petrol pumps, isn't there?

DAD: Yes. There's a tap and a fire hydrant.

DANNY: Couldn't we extend the pipe to the caravan?

DOCTOR SPENCER: The Water Board could do that with the greatest of ease.

DANNY: And couldn't we build a proper run to keep the chickens in?

CHARLIE: I'd be glad to give you a hand with that. Bit of wire, few pieces of wood. No problem.

DOCTOR SPENCER: No problem indeed. And four weeks in which to complete the work. Well, Mr Hazell?

HAZELL: It's not as simple as that.

DAD: I think it is, Mr Hazell.

DANNY: Please, Mr Hazell.
[*Pause.* HAZELL *looks around. The villagers are implacable*]

[*Suddenly* HAZELL *tears up the eviction order, temporarily defeated. He stalks out*]

[*All cheer and surround* DANNY]

MRS CLIPSTONE: Well done, Danny!

CHARLIE: That showed 'im!

DOCTOR SPENCER: I think he'll keep a low profile, for a while at least!

DAD: Thank you all for your support.

DANNY: [*To the audience*] And thank you, too! For helping save our home!
[*All applaud the audience*]

DOCTOR SPENCER: Happy, William?

DAD: Of course, Doc. But sad too.

CHARLIE: How come, Willum?

DAD: Sad that we've nothing to show from Danny's brilliant Sleeping Beauty Method! We deserved just a few spoils, didn't we?
[*The others laugh*]

MRS CLIPSTONE: I wish now I hadn't delivered them in Christopher's pram!

DAD: Christopher. Is he all right?

MRS CLIPSTONE: Sleeping like a baby.

DANNY: Well, he *is* a baby!

DOCTOR SPENCER: You know . . . I have a hunch!

CHARLIE: What sort of a hunch, Doc?

DOCTOR SPENCER: Don't you think some of the

pheasants might have been greedier than the others? Might have gobbled up more than their share of raisins?

DAD: We did think of that. Eh, Danny?

DANNY: Yes.

DOCTOR SPENCER: I wonder, Mrs Clipstone, would you mind terribly if I asked you to lift Christopher out of his pram for me?

MRS CLIPSTONE: As long as he doesn't wake up!
    [*She carefully lifts the baby out.* DOCTOR SPENCER *pounces on the pram, and lifts out some pheasants*]

DOCTOR SPENCER: I knew it! I don't think these will *ever* wake up.

DAD: Aha! Marvellous, Doc. How about two each?
    [*He starts to hand them round. General delight*]

    [*Enter* SERGEANT SAMWAYS]

With our sincere and grateful thanks!

SERGEANT SAMWAYS: Hello! What's all this then?
    [DAD *turns and sees* SERGEANT SAMWAYS. *The others look somewhat sheepishly guilty. Does the policeman's arrival signal trouble?*]

DAD: [*Approaching*] Sergeant! You're just in time!
    [*He hands him two pheasants*]

SERGEANT SAMWAYS: [*After a pause – how will he react?*] My, my, Willum. [*Accepting the pheasants*] You've come up trumps this time!
[*Everyone relaxes*]

DAD: Thanks to Danny!

SERGEANT SAMWAYS: Thanks, Danny!

ALL: Thanks, Danny!
[*As everybody divides the spoils, saying their thank-yous and goodbyes,* DANNY *comes forward and talks to the audience*]

DANNY: It's great living in a village. Sharing the good times. Helping each other through the bad times. I expect Mr Hazell will rear his ugly head again someday, but I think we're safe for now.
[*All except* DAD *exit, as* DAD *joins* DANNY]

DAD: Thanks, Danny. Your mum would be proud of you.

DANNY: And of you.

DAD: [*Smiling*] I've done my best.

DANNY: Are we a team from now on?

DAD: The best team. Top of the league!

DANNY: No more secrets?

DAD: No more secrets.

DANNY: Except poaching secrets.

DAD: Just between us!

DANNY: You know what, Dad?

DAD: What?

DANNY: You're sparky! I like that. Not everyone's dad is sparky.

DAD: And not every dad has a son who's the Champion, not of the Village, not of the County – DANNY, THE CHAMPION OF THE WORLD!
   [*They hug*]

[*Curtain down*]

GIPSY CARAVAN

A sky-blue gipsy caravan has stood in the garden of Gipsy House – where Roald Dahl wrote many of his most famous books – since 1960. It became the setting for *Danny the Champion of the World*.

Roald originally bought the caravan for his children to play in. Once, it caught fire and Roald had to put out the flames with his garden hose!

Roald's children had great fun playing in the caravan – sometimes they even camped out in it, having adventures of their own, just like Danny.

MORE ABOUT
Danny the Champion of the World

OPHELIA

Roald Dahl's daughter Ophelia was just like Danny, learning to drive a car when she was very young. Roald taught her in the orchard of Gipsy House when she was only ten years old. A few months later, the mischievous Ophelia borrowed the car, drove to the local village to buy sweets, but got stuck when the car broke down. Sheepishly, she phoned her father to be rescued, but Roald was more annoyed that she'd interrupted his writing than by her under-age driving!

WAGGLE YOUR EARS

Or, as the BFG would say, *swiggle* your ears and listen to your favourite Roald Dahl story in your room, in the car, on your way to school or the zoo or to buy chocolate . . .

Listen and laugh as **top-name actors**, including Richard E. Grant, Joanna Lumley, Simon Callow and Jeremy Irons, bring your best-loved Roald Dahl moments to life.

OUT NOW on Puffin Audio

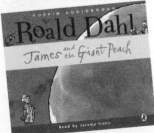

THERE'S MORE TO ROALD DAHL THAN GREAT STORIES . . .

Did you know that 10% of Roald Dahl's royalties* from this book go to help the work of the Roald Dahl charities?

Roald Dahl's Marvellous Children's Charity exists to make life better for seriously ill children because it believes that every child has the right to a marvellous life.

This marvellous charity helps thousands of children each year living with serious conditions of the blood and the brain – causes important to Roald Dahl in his lifetime – whether by providing nurses, equipment or toys for today's children in the UK, or helping tomorrow's children everywhere through pioneering research.

Can you do something marvellous to help others? Find out how at **www.marvellouschildrenscharity.org**

The Roald Dahl Museum and Story Centre, based in Great Missenden just outside London, is in the Buckinghamshire village where Roald Dahl lived and wrote. At the heart of the Museum, created to inspire a love of reading and writing, is his unique archive of letters and manuscripts. As well as two fun-packed biographical galleries, the Museum boasts an interactive Story Centre. It is a place for the family, teachers and their pupils to explore the exciting world of creativity and literacy.

Find out more at **www.roalddahlmuseum.org**

Roald Dahl's Marvellous Children's Charity (RDMCC) is a registered charity no. 1137409.

The Roald Dahl Museum and Story Centre (RDMSC) is a registered charity no. 1085853.

The Roald Dahl Charitable Trust is a registered charity no. 1119330 and supports the work of RDMCC and RDMSC.

* Donated royalties are net of commission

It all started with a Scarecrow

Puffin is well over sixty years old.
Sounds ancient, doesn't it? But Puffin has never been
so lively. We're always on the lookout for the next big
idea, which is how it began all those years ago.

Penguin Books was a big idea from the mind of
a man called Allen Lane, who in 1935 invented
the quality paperback and changed the world.
**And from great Penguins, great Puffins grew,
changing the face of children's books forever.**

The first four Puffin Picture Books were hatched in 1940 and the
first Puffin story book featured a man with broomstick arms called
Worzel Gummidge. In 1967 Kaye Webb, Puffin Editor, started the
Puffin Club, promising to **'make children into readers'.**
She kept that promise and over 200,000 children became
devoted Puffineers through their quarterly instalments of
Puffin Post, which is now back for a new generation.

Many years from now, we hope you'll look back and
remember Puffin with a smile. **No matter what your age
or what you're into, there's a Puffin for everyone.**
The possibilities are endless, but one thing is for sure:
whether it's a picture book or a paperback, a sticker book
or a hardback, **if it's got that little Puffin
on it – it's bound to be good.**